FINISH LINE

Reading

for the Common Core State Standards

Continental

Acknowledgments

Illustrations: Pages 17, 183: Sally Springer; Pages 27, 41, 69, 75, 107, 116, 136, 148, 164, 171, 182, 186, 187, 204: Laurie Conley; Pages 31, 47, 55, 58, 175, 197: Margaret Lindmark; Page 44: Marty Hustead; Page 132: Jane Yamada; Page 147: John Norton; Page 148: Estella Hickman; Page 156: Cindy Shaw; Page 195: Marilee Harrald-Pilz

Photographs: Page 8: Corbis; Page 9: www.photos.com; Page 15: NASA; Page 21: CMCD, Inc.; Page 23: www.istockphoto.com/birdimages; Page 29: Corbis; Page 37: www.photos.com; Page 48: Image used under Creative Commons from Wolfgang 1018; Page 52: Image used under Creative Commons from Solid State Survivor; Page 92: AP photo by Tom Strattman; Page 96: www.shutterstock.com, Fouquin; Page 102: Library of Congress, Prints and Photographs Division, LC-USZ62-10598; Page 124: Image used under Creative Commons from Rico Shen; Page 140: Courtesy of National Archives and Records Administration; Page 152: Courtesy of Team Romero; Page 159: www.istockphoto.com/Ralph125; Page 160: www.istockphoto.com/YaleBernstein; Page 160: www.istockphoto.com/thebroker; Page 174: Fine Line Photography; Page 193: Treadwell & Peaslee

Table of Contents

Welcome to Finish Line Reading for the Common Core State Standards

This book will give you practice in the reading and comprehension skills necessary to be an effective reader. It will also help you to prepare for reading tests that assess your skills and knowledge.

The material in this book is aligned to the Common Core State Standards for English Language Arts and Literacy in History, Social Studies, Science, and Technical Subjects. The Common Core State Standards (CCSS) build on the education standards developed by the states. The CCSS "specify what literacy skills and understandings are required for college and career readiness in multiple disciplines." This book will help you practice the skills necessary to be a literate person in the 21st century.

In the lessons of this book, you will read informational and literary selections and then answer multiple-choice and short-response questions about them. The lessons in this book are in three parts:

- The first part introduces the reading skill you are going to study and explains what it is and how you use it.

- The second part is called Guided Practice. You will get more than just practice here; you will get help. You will read a story, poem, or nonfiction article and answer questions about it. After each question, you will find an explanation of the correct answer. So you will answer questions and find out right away if you were correct. You will also learn why one answer is correct and others are not.

- The third part is called Test Yourself. Here you will read a passage and answer the questions on your own.

When you finish each unit, you will complete a Review Lesson to show what you have learned in that unit. This will help you evaluate the progress you are making. After you have finished all of the lessons and units, you will take a Practice Test at the end of the book.

Now you are ready to begin using this book. Good Luck!

Vocabulary Development

It all begins with words. You may be reading, writing, or talking. You're using words all the time. When you think, you do so mainly in words. Words are even used while dreaming. You need words!

It makes sense, then, to learn as many words as you can.

You already know a lot of words. There are many that you use when you talk. Yet, there are many more that you can understand when you read them. This unit is all about vocabulary development— learning the meanings of new words and how to use them.

● **In Lesson 1,** you'll learn about context clues, or how to figure out the meanings of new words when you read them. You will do this by relating them to the words in the sentence or paragraph that you already know. Sometimes words will have more than one meaning. You will learn how to tell which meaning of a word is meant. Finally, you'll add new words to your vocabulary by adding extra parts to words you already know.

● **Lesson 2** is all about words that don't mean exactly what they say. You'll learn about figurative language. That is, you will learn words that writers use to express ideas in new and different ways. You'll learn about idioms, adages, and proverbs. These are phrases that mean something quite different from the actual words in them. And you'll learn how to figure out the meanings of words that mean and sound like *almost* the same thing.

● **Lesson 3** is about those words that you may not use in conversation. You may not even find them in your regular reading. Yet, these words will become important to know when you're reading about science, social studies, or other subjects. You'll learn how to use context clues to discover the meanings of special terms.

Now turn the page and start building your vocabulary!

Word Meanings

L.4.4, RL.4.4, RI.4.4

Try to think back to when you were very young. You did not know many words. So, you listened to others speak. Perhaps, you may have pointed and asked, "What's that?" Others answered, "That's a car," or "That's a tree." But mostly you learned new words by hearing people use them. You learned from adults, from other children, even from TV and songs. You figured out what words mean by the way they related, or connected, to the words you already know. You learned new words by using **context clues.**

When you were very young, you had to rely on listening to learn new words. However, now you are older and can read. When you were younger, you used context clues to figure out the meaning of new words you heard. Now, you have to figure out the meaning of new words that you read using context clues in sentences or paragraphs.

Context Clues

Read these sentences from *Pinocchio,* by Carlo Collodi.

While Pinocchio swam fast so as to reach the beach quickly, he perceived that his papa, who sat on his back, trembled just as if he had a high fever. Did he tremble from cold or fear? Who knows? Perhaps, a little of both.

Do you know what the word <u>perceived</u> means? If you don't, you can figure out its meaning. Look at the words and ideas around the word. You have two context clues. First, because the word ends in *-ed*, you know it's a past tense verb. Pinocchio did something. The second clue is in the sentence and the next one. Pinocchio felt his father tremble. Pinocchio must have been feeling, or sensing, something. You can guess that the word <u>perceived</u> means "noticed" or "observed" through the senses.

Context clues may come in several forms:

Context Clues

Synonyms	Words that have nearly the same meanings
Examples	Words that show what another word means
Definitions	Words that tell what another word means
Descriptions	Words that tell you more about a word, such as by comparing or by explaining an action it causes

Synonyms

Sometimes you can find words in the sentence or paragraph that mean nearly the same thing. If you know one word, then you can figure out the other.

We walked from class to class distributing the boxes, making sure that we were giving them to the right owners.

The words distributing and giving both explain the act of handing something out. Even if you didn't know the meaning of distributing, you could figure out from the context that it means basically the same as giving.

Examples

Other times you can figure out what words mean through examples. There may be an unknown word. Then there will be an example of the unknown word to help you understand.

Jane Goodall is probably the most famous primatologist in history. She has spent over 45 years studying monkeys in the wild.

What does primatologist mean? The context shows that it's a noun. The -ologist ending suggests that it's a kind of scientist. The example explains how she has spent more than 45 years studying monkeys. You can figure out that primatologist means "a scientist who studies monkeys."

Definitions

An unknown word is sometimes defined in context. Look for a definition in these sentences:

> Annie's teacher gave her a confidential letter to take home to her parents. The teacher told her not to reveal the contents to anyone but her mom and dad. Once Annie got home, she took out the letter and shared it together in private with her parents.

You may or may not have heard the word <u>confidential</u>. You can tell that the word is an adjective because it describes the letter. However, the paragraph gives you the definition. The context tells you that <u>confidential</u> means "to be shared together in private."

Descriptions

Sentences may contain a description to tell you what a word means. The description might *compare* something you know. Or, it might show you a *connection* between the new word and the one you know.

> Although Peter missed many baskets, we reassured him of his worth. We all supported him with high fives and encouragement.

You may not know the word <u>reassured</u>, but you can tell by comparison with *supported* and *encouragement* that it means "helping."

> The world's largest predatory shark is the great white. It has strong jaws, rows of bone-cutting teeth, and attacks dolphins and whales.

The word <u>predatory</u> may be new to you. However, you can figure out what it means. Look at the descriptions of the shark. The descriptions are "strong jaws, rows of bone-cutting teeth, and attacks dolphins and whales." You could use these descriptions to understand that <u>predatory</u> means "killing and eating other animals."

Guided Practice

Imagine that you find a large rocky area. In it you find a dinosaur <u>fossil</u>. You want to know how old this <u>relic</u> is because you would like to sell it to a museum. You will have to use a special high-tech way of finding out the date. Scientists use <u>carbon dating</u>. This is how it works. All living things breathe and eat. When they do this, they take in something called carbon-14. When living things die, the carbon-14 is still in their bodies. The older the fossils are, the less carbon-14 there is trapped in the rock. Scientists can then <u>estimate</u> when a dinosaur lived by how much carbon-14 is in the fossil.

Check the exact meaning of the new words in this passage by checking their meaning in a print or online dictionary.

The word <u>fossil</u> means _____.

A   something that is tested

B   a high-tech way of dating rocks

C   bones from dinosaurs

D   remains of something that lived

If you do not know what a <u>fossil</u> is, you can figure it out through the descriptions. The first sentence talks about rocky land, so you know that a fossil has something to do with rocks. You also think it has something to do with dinosaurs. Yet, you read that all living things can make fossils, so fossils may be a larger term for the remains of something that lived. You can conclude that the correct answer is choice D.

The word <u>relic</u> means _____.

  A something old

  B up for sale

  C exhibit

  D animal bone

> You need to use synonyms to answer this question. First, figure out what the word <u>fossil</u> means from the context clues. After you figure this out, you will notice that relic is just a different word choice for the word <u>fossil</u>. A <u>relic</u> is "something old." The correct answer is choice A.

An <u>estimate</u> means the same as _____.

  A a rumor

  B an opinion

  C a good guess

  D an actual time

> Understanding this word involves making a comparison in your mind. Imagine you could measure the carbon-14. It would be impossible to know exactly how old the fossil would be. You would just be guessing. However, it is more than an opinion because you have the measured carbon-14. It would probably be a good guess that you would make. The correct answer is choice C.

<u>Carbon dating</u> is a science term in the passage. Using all the information in the passage, how would you explain this term?

_____

_____

> You need to look at the entire paragraph to understand what carbon dating is used for and what it is. Here's a sample answer:

  Carbon dating is a way of figuring out how old a fossil is by finding out how much carbon-14 is left in the rock.

UNIT 1 ▚▚▚▚▚▚▚▚▚▚▚▚▚▚▚▚▚▚▚▚▚▚▚▚▚▚▚▚▚▚▚▚▚▚▚▚▚
Vocabulary Development

Words With Multiple Meanings

    Words can be tricky. Some words can have more than one meaning. A dictionary will list each meaning separately. Usually, the dictionary will have numbers in front of the different meanings. Most of the time, the different meanings are spelled and even pronounced alike. If you don't know all the meanings, you may not understand what you're reading. Here are some of the many meanings of the word <u>root</u>:

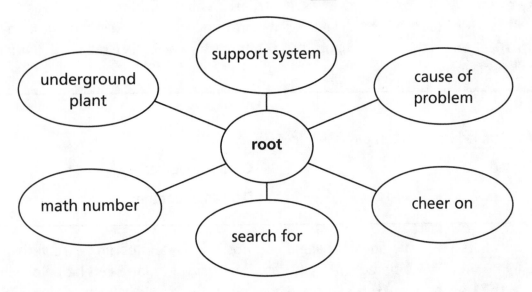

    When you come across a word like <u>root</u> in a sentence, use context clues to find its meaning. First, notice how the word is used in the sentence. What part of speech is it? Is it a verb (action word), a noun (the name of a person, place, or thing), or an adjective (a word that describes)?

> **Whenever he is up to bat, the fans <u>root</u> for him.**

    You can tell in this sentence that <u>root</u> is a verb. Which of the meanings shown above are verbs? There are two of them. Substitute each meaning for the word <u>root</u> in the sentence. The one that makes the most sense is "cheer on."

Guided Practice

Read the passage. Then answer the questions.

    Early humans made roads by following animal tracks. The ancient Romans were the first to <u>construct</u> roads. Romans <u>assembled</u> more than 52,988 miles of roads that all led to the center of the city. Not all roads lead to Rome anymore. In fact, there are streets, roads, highways, and superhighways that can <u>lead</u> you all over the world.

The word <u>construct</u> in this passage means ____.

A build

B idea

C compose

D thought

As used in the passage, the word <u>construct</u> is a verb. You can cross off choices B and D, which are both noun forms of the word. In its noun form, the word is even said differently (CON•struct). Which of the other choices are verbs? "Compose" doesn't make sense in this context. The word *made* in the first sentence gives you a clue that the best answer is "build." Choice A is the correct answer.

What does <u>assembled</u> mean in this passage?

A collected

B gathered

C put together

D came together

<u>Assembled</u> may have any of these meanings. All these meanings are verbs. The clue words in the paragraph, such as *construct* and *made* can help you decide the best answer. You can start swapping out words. Which of these questions make sense? Did Romans collect roads? Gather roads? Put together roads? Come together roads? Choice C is the correct answer.

What does the word <u>lead</u> mean in this passage? Explain your answer.

_____

_____

_____

_____

Here is a sample answer:

<u>Lead</u> means "to guide and direct towards a place." In this passage, <u>lead</u> is used as a verb. As a verb, <u>lead</u> could mean "to guide," "to be in charge of," or "to be winning." In this context, the best answer means "to guide."

Using Prefixes, Suffixes, and Root Words _____

Sometimes you might recognize parts of a word. You often can learn new words because you already know smaller parts. A **prefix** is a part of a word added to the beginning of the word that changes the meaning of the word. If you know the word <u>friendly</u>, and you know that the prefix *un-* means "not," you can figure out that <u>unfriendly</u> means "not friendly."

A **suffix** is a part added to the end of a word that changes the meaning of the word. If you know the word <u>thought</u>, and you know that the suffix *-less* means "without," you can figure out that <u>thoughtless</u> means "without thought."

Most prefixes and suffixes come from Latin and Greek words. For example, the prefix *tri-* comes from the Latin word for "three." This prefix probably came from the Greek god called "Triton" who lived under the sea. Some say he had a *trident*, which is like a pitchfork with three tines. Think of the word *tricycle*. It has three wheels!

Some Common Prefixes

Prefix	Meaning	Example
bi-	two	<u>bi</u>cycle
dis-	not	<u>dis</u>agree
ex-	from, away from	<u>ex</u>hale
in-	in or not	<u>in</u>expensive
mid-	middle	<u>mid</u>way
mis-	bad or not	<u>mis</u>behave
pre-	before	<u>pre</u>view
re-	back, again	<u>re</u>play
sub-	under, less than	<u>sub</u>way
super-	over, high, higher	<u>super</u>star
un-	not	<u>un</u>kind
uni-	one	<u>uni</u>form

Some Common Suffixes

Suffix	Meaning	Example
-able	able to	comfort<u>able</u>
-ful	full of, likely to	rest<u>ful</u>
-ish	being like	child<u>ish</u>
-less	without	humor<u>less</u>
-ly	like, in the manner of	usual<u>ly</u>
-ment	the act of or result	enjoy<u>ment</u>
-or	a person who	invent<u>or</u>
-y	like or tending to	stick<u>y</u>

Prefixes and suffixes may be added to **root words** to make new words. If you know the meaning of a root word, it helps. If you know the meaning of a prefix or suffix, you can usually figure out the meaning of new words.

Many English words come from Greek and Latin. For instance, the Latin root <u>act</u> means "to do or drive." From the suffix list, you know that -*or* means "a person who." The word <u>actor</u> means "someone who acts out."

Some Common Greek and Latin Roots

Root Word	Meaning	New Word	New Word Meaning
auto	self	automobile	self-moving
aqua	water	aquarium	water-filled container
bio	life	biography	writing about someone's life
geo	earth	geography	study of the earth
graph	write, draw	autograph	self-writing
log	study	zoology	animal study
mar	sea	marsh	a wet, grassy area

Guided Practice

Jacques Cousteau is one of the most famous marine biologists of all time. He lived from 1910–1997. During this time, he studied the ocean. He was a skillful swimmer and invented a way to dive underwater for longer length of times. He called it the aqualung. Today, we call it scuba diving. During his life, he used a movie camera to film subaquatic life. He shared all his knowledge in books and film. In fact, he had a TV series that lasted nine years. Many people were able to see ocean floor animals, as well as sharks and dolphins for the first time.

The title marine biologist means a person who _____.

A studies life in water

B studies all life

C writes about life

D who lives in water

You know that the root mar means "water." You know that *bio* means "life." You know that *-log* is the "study of something." If you put these together, you have someone who studies water life. Choice A is the correct answer.

What do you think an <u>aqualung</u> would be?

_____

_____

 A look at the root word chart shows you that the root <u>aqua</u> means "water." You already know that you use your lungs to breathe. You might also know what scuba diving is. Here is a sample answer:

An <u>aqualung</u> is a machine that allows someone to breathe in the water.

What does <u>subaquatic</u> mean?

A under water

B over water

C full of water

D lacking water

 Since you know what <u>aqua</u> means, you can find the prefix *sub-* on the prefix list. If you forgot what *sub-* means, you could think of common words, like *submarine*. This word means "under the sea." You could probably guess that <u>subaquatic</u> would mean something similar.

Test Yourself

Did you know that we are living in the Cenozoic Era? This era began 65,000 million years ago! It was a time of new life. Before this time, all large animals had become <u>extinct</u>. All <u>giant</u> dinosaurs died out except for dinosaur birds. All land animals larger than crocodiles had <u>disappeared</u>. Many smaller animals and birds had <u>sustained</u>, and continued to <u>thrive</u>.

At the beginning of the Cenozoic Era, Earth was like a greenhouse. It was warm and humid on the planet. Scientists think that forests even covered the North and South Poles.

Slowly, things started to cool and become chilly. Ice began forming on quite a bit of the planet. Brr! Yet, soon the ice <u>thawed</u>. The grasslands grew again. The animals that <u>endured</u> the cold times were able to graze on the land again.

One of the animals that was able to survive until more recently was the woolly mammoth. Scientists think that woolly mammoths lived 800,000 years ago. Mammoths are <u>comparable</u> to the size of an elephant. But mammoths had smaller ears and a shaggy coat to keep them warm. Like elephants, mammoths moved in herds. They <u>flourished</u> on grasses and low plants. Just 6,000 years ago they all died out.

There have been many changes during this era. Yet, many animals were close relatives to the animals that live on our planet now.

1 The word <u>extinct</u> means ____.

   A exit

   B active

   C died out

   D still living

2 What does <u>disappeared</u> mean?

   A not showing

   B not working

   C coming out

   D showing up

3 Sustained means ____.

    A measured

    B passed on

    C continued

    D for a moment

4 What does it mean to thrive?

    A grow

    B weaken

    C get worse

    D stay the same

5 In paragraph 3, the word thawed means ____.

    A boil

    B melt

    C freeze up

    D become solid

6 The word endured means ____.

    A died

    B departed

    C carried on

    D slipped away

7 What does comparable mean in paragraph 4?

    A copy

    B alike

    C unalike

    D different

8 As used in this article, the word <u>flourished</u> means _____.

   A grew

   B weakened

   C became ill

   D stayed the same

9 Explain your answer to question 8.

_____

_____

_____

_____

_____

Read the passage. Then answer the question.

In Greek mythology, the Giants were huge, violent creatures. The Giants later attacked the Olympian gods. The Giants were defeated and imprisoned under the earth. The early Greeks said that whenever a volcano erupts, then a giant is hidden.

10 Explain the possible reasons why we still use the word <u>giant</u> today.

_____

_____

_____

_____

_____

Word Relationships

L.4.5, RL.4.4, RI.4.4

Words can have more than one meaning. For example, read the following sentence: Words can have shades of meaning. The word *shades* is one of those words with multiple meanings. It can mean something you put over windows. It can mean lightness or darkness of color. It can even mean sunglasses. What does this have to do with words?

Figurative Language

We are using **figurative language** when we say that words have shades of meaning. Writers use figurative language to appeal to your senses. This helps you see, feel, hear, or understand things more vividly. "The snow fell" is a literal statement. It simply tells you about the weather. "The snow fell like popcorn from the sky" lets you *see* the snow as it falls. The next sentence lets you *feel* the snow. "The snow was a soft white cub cuddling with its mother." Finally, read the next sentence and see if you can hear the snow. "The snow fell like whispers on a mountain."

"The snow fell like whispers on a mountain" is one type of figurative language. It is called a **simile** (SIM•uh•lee). A simile uses the word *like* or *as* to compare two things. Usually, it compares two unlike things. This simile lets you hear the softness of the snow as it falls.

A **metaphor** (MET•uh•for) is like a simile. It also compares two unlike things, but it does not use the word *like* or *as*. "The snow was a soft white cub cuddling with its mother." This shows a relationship between two unlike objects.

"The snow fell like whispers on a mountain" is also another type of figurative language. It is called **personification.** Using this, a writer gives human traits to a nonliving thing. In this case, the mountain is whispering. We know a mountain cannot whisper. The writer is trying to make the mountain seem more alive.

Figurative language is important to understand. If you mistake what the writer is trying to do, you might miss the writer's meaning.

Elements of Poetry

You will find rich figurative language in **poetry.** Many poets like to paint word pictures. Often, this is done through the senses. A poem's **theme**—the main idea that the poet wants you to understand—is often told in figurative language.

There are many different kinds of poems. **Narrative poems** tell a story. **Lyric poems** mainly explain feelings. There are many forms of poems as well. **Ballads** are narrative poems that are written to be sung. A **haiku** is a Japanese poem that has exactly 17 syllables and is about nature. A **limerick** is an English poem that has five lines and is meant for fun.

Every poem has a **speaker.** The speaker in the poem gives ideas and a point of view. Sometimes the speaker is the poet, and sometimes it is a made-up character.

Many poems have **rhyme**—repeated sounds at the ends of words. Sometimes the rhyme comes at the ends of a line of poetry, as in this limerick by Edward Lear:

> *There was an Old Man with a beard,*
> *Who said, 'It is just as I feared!*
> *Two Owls and a Hen,*
> *Four Larks and a Wren,*
> *Have all built their nests in my beard!'*

Sometimes rhyming words appear in the same line:

> *There was a little **girl** who had a little **curl***

Many poems have no rhyme at all, like this **haiku:**

Beautiful turtle,
Climb up the highest mountain,
But do it slowly.

Rhythm is the pattern of beats. Imagine if you played a drum with all hard beats. Your song may not be enjoyable. In poems, there are stressed and unstressed beats. Many poems have the same beat pattern. A stressed beat has more force than an unstressed beat.

> It's **rai**ning, it's **pour**ing,
> The **old** man is **snor**ing;
> He **went** to **bed** and **bumped** his **head**
> And **couldn't** get **up** in the **morning**!

Some poems do not have rhyme or a regular rhythm. These poems are called **free verse.**

> The sun beaming its rays of golden yellow,
> Blissfully mixing with the prisms of heavenly tears,
> Look in the sky—an arch of colors.

Poets also use other tools besides figurative language. Poets can use the *sounds* of words. These can be playful or meaningful. Poets sometimes repeat the same beginning consonant sound in a line. This is called **alliteration.** In this first line, we hear the /g/ sound repeated. In the second, we heard the /w/ sound. Both are examples of alliteration:

> *Grey goose and gander,*
> *Waft your wings together,*

Another way poets play with sounds is called **onomatopoeia.** Words that imitate the sound of something, such as *boom, crash,* and *cluck,* are examples of onomatopoeia.

Writers break up thoughts into paragraphs. Poets may divide lines into **stanzas.** These are groups of lines separated by spaces. The poem on the next page has two stanzas.

Guided Practice

The Eagle

by Alfred, Lord Tennyson

He clasps the crag¹ with crooked hands;
Close to the sun in lonely lands,
Ring'd with the azure² world, he stands.

The wrinkled sea beneath him crawls;
5 He watches from his mountain walls,
And like a thunderbolt he falls.

Which line from the poem includes a simile?

A He clasps the crag with crooked hands;

B Ring'd with the azure world, he stands.

C The wrinkled sea beneath him crawls;

D And like a thunderbolt he falls.

The poet uses a lot of figurative language in this poem. Yet, there is only one simile. Choice D is the correct answer. Tennyson uses the word *like* to compare the way the eagle falls to a thunderbolt.

In line 1, what is the speaker referring to when he says "crooked hands"?

A his own hands

B the bird's feet

C the birds wings

D the form of the rock

Since the poem is titled, "The Eagle," the pronoun *He* is referring to the bird. Imagine what this eagle looks like on top of a tall rock. It would hold, or "clasp," the rock with its "crooked hands." Since birds do not have hands, we can guess that the poet means the bird's claws, or feet. Choice B is the correct answer.

---

¹**crag:** steep mass of jagged rock

²**azure:** blue, referring to the sky

"The wrinkled sea beneath him crawls" is an example of ____.

A simile

B metaphor

C onomatopoeia

D personification

> ✓ The eagle looks down from the tall rock at the waves in the water, or "wrinkled sea." We know that water cannot crawl like a person can. This is an example of personification. Choice D is the correct answer.

Write a line from the poem that uses alliteration.

_____

_____

> ✓ Alliteration is the repetition of a consonant sound in a line of poetry. Here is a sample answer:

"He clasps the crag with crooked hands" is the correct answer.
The poet uses alliteration with the /c/ sound in line 1.

What words in the poem help you see and feel how strong the eagle is?

_____

_____

> ✓ There is no single correct answer to a question like this. Try to picture in your mind the scene the poet describes. Here is one sample answer:

The poet uses "crag," and I could feel the height and hardness.
He also uses the sound of a thunderbolt to show the eagle's power.

Idioms, Adages, and Proverbs ⎯⎯⎯⎯⎯⎯⎯⎯⎯⎯⎯⎯⎯

Idioms are another kind of figurative language. An idiom is a phrase in which the words have nothing to do with their actual meanings. For example, it may be raining so hard that we describe it as raining cats and dogs. Of course, cats and dogs are not falling from the sky. The meaning of the phrase has nothing to do with the literal meanings of *cats* or *dogs*.

Here are some other familiar idioms:

Idiom	Meaning
hit the hay	go to sleep
green thumb	special talent for growing plants
monkey business	fooling around
on the ball	alert and skillful

Idioms develop over time. Usually, there is a story behind them. For example, the saying hit the hay began in the 1930s when there were many people without homes. Often, these people would find shelter in a barn. As soon as their heads hit the hay, they were asleep. One of the oldest idioms is open Pandora's box. This idiom is based on the Greek myth in which the god Zeus gave Pandora a box and told her not to open it. She opened it anyway, and all the evils of the world came out. The only good left in the box was "hope."

Can you think of some other idioms? Write a few on the lines below.

Idiom	**Meaning**
_____	_____
_____	_____
_____	_____
_____	_____
_____	_____

Adages and **proverbs** are short "wise sayings." They are like idioms, but they are a little more important. They may explain useful or basic truths. Sometimes they are repeated so many times that people forget their literal meanings.

Here are some familiar adages and proverbs. Can you see the metaphor in each of them?

Adage or Proverb	Meaning
Never look a gift horse in the mouth.	Accept what is given to you without questioning it.
A stitch in time saves nine.	Repair something before it gets worse.
Blood is thicker than water.	Family is more important than other relationships.
Getting out on the wrong side of the bed.	Waking up in a bad mood.
He who asks is a fool for five minutes. He who never asks is a fool for a lifetime.	If you don't ask questions when you don't know something, you will never learn.
If you don't want anyone to know, don't do it.	If you are ashamed of doing something, then don't do it at all.

Write a few more adages and proverbs that you have heard.

Adage or Proverb	**Meaning**
_____	_____
_____	_____
_____	_____
_____	_____
_____	_____

Guided Practice

My aunt put a bowl on the table before me.

"What is this strange-smelling green soup?" I asked my aunt.

"Oh, <u>don't judge a book by its cover</u>. Just try it," she said.

"Okay, here it goes," I said as I put the spoonful of soup into my mouth and swallowed.

The soup was terrible, but I didn't want to tell my aunt.

"What do you think?" my aunt asked.

I just nodded my head as if I were saying "yes," but I clammed up, and just buttoned my lip.

My aunt laughed, "What's wrong? <u>Cat got your tongue?</u> You can make a sandwich for yourself if you don't like it."

What does the adage <u>don't judge a book by its cover</u> mean in this passage?

A   Don't make up your mind before trying something.

B   Don't try it until you make up your mind about something.

C   Try something but don't judge it.

D   Try something but don't like it.

<u>Don't judge a book by its cover</u> is an adage that means not to judge the inside of something by its outside. Or, don't judge something by its appearance. The aunt was saying not to judge the soup before trying it. The correct answer is choice A.

What is the meaning of the adage <u>cat got your tongue</u>?

_____

_____

> ✓ The context should tell you what this old adage means. The aunt made the boy try his soup, but he doesn't like it. He doesn't say anything because he does not want to be rude. Here is a sample answer:

> If someone asks if the <u>cat got your tongue</u>, he is asking why you are so quiet.

What are two other idioms in the passage? Explain what they mean.

_____

_____

_____

_____

> ✓ The two other idioms in the passage are "clammed up" and "buttoned my lip." Here is a sample answer:

> It is hard to pry open a clam's shell. The idiom <u>clammed up</u> means that you are not showing your feelings or telling someone what is wrong. The idiom <u>buttoned my lip</u> means that you are keeping your mouth tightly closed and not saying anything.

Word Relationships

Words can be compared and contrasted to other words. **Synonyms** are words that have almost the same meaning. But there can be a lot of difference in that "almost." Consider the adjective <u>clever</u>. The word describes a person who is intelligent. No one would be offended by being called intelligent. However, consider these synonyms: <u>sly</u>, <u>trickster</u>, <u>wily</u>, and <u>savvy</u>. How would you feel about a person described by any of those words?

> Make sure you know the exact meaning and pronunciation of these synonyms by looking them up in a print or online dictionary.

Antonyms are words that have opposite meanings to one another. Again, consider <u>clever</u> and its synonyms as you read these sentences:

> He was so <u>childish</u> when he played with his toy train.
>
> He was so <u>youthful</u> when he played with his toy train.

Both <u>childish</u> and <u>youthful</u> can describe someone who is not clever. However, think about what they mean. <u>Childish</u> is an antonym of <u>clever</u>. Yet, <u>childish</u> is a negative quality. <u>Youthful</u> can also be an antonym of <u>sly</u> and <u>savvy</u>. However, it describes what most people would consider a positive quality.

Homographs are words that are spelled the same but that have different meanings. They can also have different pronunciations depending on how they are used. For example, <u>fine</u> is a homograph. It can mean a <u>fine</u> that you pay or that you are feeling <u>fine</u>. It's important not to confuse a word with its homograph when you come across it as you read.

Guided Practice

Read the poem. Then answer the questions.

The Rainbow

by Christina Rossetti

Boats <u>sail</u> on the rivers,
And ships sail on the seas;
But clouds that sail across the sky
Are prettier far than these.
5 There are <u>bridges</u> on the rivers,
As pretty as you <u>please</u>;
But the bow that <u>bridges</u> heaven,
And overtops the trees,
And builds a road from earth to sky,
10 Is prettier far than these.

Which word would best replace <u>sail</u> in line 1?

A charge

B glide

C tear

D rush

All these verbs represent different movements. We have to figure out what the best synonym of <u>sail</u> would be. "Charge, tear," and "rush" do not suggest moving slowly across the water. Choices A, C, and D are incorrect. Choice B is the correct answer.

Which word is an antonym of <u>please</u> in line 6?

A like

B annoy

C entertained

D thrill

"Like" is a synonym for <u>please</u> in this context. So, we can cross that one out. The most opposite word, or antonym, of <u>please</u> is "annoy." Choice B is the correct answer.

The word <u>bridges</u> is used two different ways in lines 5 and 7. Explain the homographs in this sentence.

_____

_____

_____

Here is one way to answer the question:

In line 5, the word <u>bridges</u> is a noun. It means "a structure that crosses over something, such as a river, to get to the other side." In line 7, the word <u>bridges</u> is a verb. It means "connects."

Test Yourself

My brother, mom, grandma, and I were tucked into our sleeping bags in our large tent. I pretended to <u>sleep like a baby</u>. Yet, I still wanted to finish the book I was reading. When I heard everyone snoring, I took out my flashlight, got some juice and <u>cereal</u> from the cooler outside, and started to read in my sleeping bag.

I was at a really good part of the book when I heard a growling sound. My <u>heart pounded like heavy knocks on a door</u>. My entire body was a <u>statue, still and silent</u>.

As I moved my flashlight towards the wall of the tent, I saw a large creature. It had our cooler open. All I heard was a steady *Grrrrrrr*. Was it a monster? I had to <u>get to the bottom of this</u>.

Since I could not fight the monster alone, I woke up grandma.

"Grandma, there is a monster outside in the cooler!"

"<u>The only thing we have to fear is fear itself</u>," Grandma yelled a little startled.

"Yes, it is eating all our food, and then it will eat us!" I yelled.

Then my mother and brother woke up. I shone the flashlight at the tent wall. "Look! It's a monster."

"It's a raccoon!" my mom exclaimed.

"Looks like we will have to catch fish for breakfast tomorrow because someone forgot to close the lid on the cooler last night," my brother added with <u>irritation</u> as he looked at me and gritted his teeth.

"Sorry!" I said <u>meekly</u>.

1 In the first sentence, the narrator pretends to <u>sleep like a baby</u>. What kind of figurative language is the narrator using?

   A simile

   B metaphor

   C onomatopoeia

   D personification

2 When the narrator explains that her heart pounded <u>like heavy knocks on a door</u>, the author wants you to understand that she was ____.

   A sad

   B calm

   C excited

   D nervous

3 In the first paragraph, the narrator uses the word <u>cereal</u>. This word actually comes from Greek mythology. From which god or goddess of grain does <u>cereal</u> *most* likely take its name?

   A Ceres

   B Cronos

   C Cupid

   D Cyclops

4 In paragraph 3, the author writes, *Grrrrrrrr.* How could you *best* describe this language?

   A adage

   B idiom

   C simile

   D onomatopoeia

5 Read this sentence from the passage.

   My entire body was a <u>statue, still and silent</u>.

This is an example of an ____.

   A adage

   B idiom

   C alliteration

   D onomatopoeia

6 In paragraph 3, what does the idiom <u>get to the bottom of this</u> mean?

_____

_____

_____

_____

7 Grandma says, "<u>The only thing we have to fear is fear itself.</u>" Explain what this means.

_____

_____

_____

_____

8 In the first paragraph, how can you tell that the word <u>cooler</u> means "container for keeping food cold" and not "to keep cool"?

_____

_____

_____

_____

9 In the second to last paragraph, the narrator's brother talks to her with <u>irritation</u>. What synonym might the narrator use for the word <u>irritation</u>?

_____

_____

_____

_____

_____

10 Explain why the narrator answers her brother <u>meekly</u> in the last line.

_____

_____

_____

_____

_____

Content-Specific Words

L.4.6, RL.4.4, RI.4.4

You learned that there are shades of words. There are also different levels of words. First, there are the words you use when you talk to your friends. These might include words that even your parents do not understand. Second, you have a polite way of talking to your teachers and parents. Third, you may notice the way authors have command over words in books or newspapers. Finally, there is specific language used for different types of reading.

For example, you use very special words in science. You may use words like *extinct* and *electricity*. In math, you may use words such as *divide* and *sum*. Social studies uses special words as well. These words might be *stagecoach* and *pony express*. In literature, we may also use words from stories, such as *titan* and *wizard*.

Guided Practice

Read the passage. Then answer the questions.

> With a small group, research other Greek myths. Present your findings to the class.

Narcissus

a retelling of a Greek myth

There was once a man named Narcissus. He was the most gorgeous man who had ever lived. The great blind seer Tiresias said that Narcissus would enjoy a long life if he never looked at his reflection. When Narcissus was 16 years old, he had already broken many hearts. He had never found anyone good enough for him.

There was a young nymph who wanted to win the heart of Narcissus. Her name was Echo. She had been punished by the jealous goddess, Hera. Echo had once been able to tell great, long stories. But now Echo could only repeat what others said to her.

Narcissus was fascinated with Echo. But he could not find her. Every time he called out, "Come over here," she could only reply, "Here, here." Narcissus asked Echo to share his heart. But all she could do was repeat his words. He grew tired of this and sent her away.

Echo was jilted and cried until she faded away. She hid in caves and mountains and still does. People can sometimes hear her voice when they speak to her in nature.

The <u>merciless</u> Narcissus who could find nobody good enough to love stopped at a river. He looked at his own reflection and fell in love with his image. When the image did not speak back to him, he tried to hug it. He explained to the image, "Every living thing loves me, why not you?" As he waited for a reply, he cried tears and finally reached out to the image in the water. He drowned, but a white flower grew near the riverside where his tears had fallen. The nymphs named the flower the narcissus.

The word <u>gorgeous</u> in this passage means a person with great _____.

   A spirit

   B beauty

   C ugliness

   D kindness

> <u>Gorgeous</u> is used to describe something of great beauty, spirit, or largeness. But this passage uses it to describe Narcissus. Since the story is about his beauty, the only answer that fits just right is choice B.

Which word is a *more* common word for <u>seer</u>?

   A friend

   B enemy

   C soothsayer

   D fortune-teller

> <u>Seer</u> is a word that you might only find in stories. You can tell from the context of the passage that Tiresias is predicting the future. We know that the word <u>seer</u> has something to do with the future. You could connect "fortune" with something that is meant to give advice about the future. "Soothsayer" means <u>seer</u>, but this is not a common word. The most common word for <u>seer</u> is "fortune-teller." Choice D is the correct answer.

What does the word <u>reflection</u> mean?

A thought

C suggest

B mirror

D sign

Here <u>reflection</u> means "mirror." Tiresias says it will be bad if Narcissus looks at his own reflection. When Narcissus does look at himself, he falls in love with the mirrorlike image he sees. Choice B is the correct answer.

Write definitions for the other underlined words in the passage. If you can't tell the meaning of the word from the context, look it up in a print or online dictionary.

nymph _____

fascinated _____

merciless _____

Did you get them all? Your answers might read something like these:

nymph—beautiful girl

fascinated— commanded interest over

merciless—easily hurts others with no feeling

Read the passage. Then answer the questions.

Bee Stinging Attacks

Did you know that bees were once used to attack enemies? The <u>ancient</u> Mayans used bees and wasps to protect themselves. The warriors waited while the enemy climbed outside ladders to attack the Mayan city. At the top of the walls, there were pretend <u>warriors</u>. A <u>dummy</u> dressed up as a warrior waited at the top of the walls. Each one had a head made from a clay pot. Can you guess what was inside the clay pot?

As the enemy attacked the dummies, the clay pots broke. Angry bees and wasps swarmed out of the clay pots and attacked the enemy. The men were frightened and many were stung more than once. They jumped off the ladders to protect themselves and ran away. The Mayan king and warriors would then celebrate their victory in their <u>fortress</u>. The bees had driven away the enemy.

The Mayans were not the only group that used bees to attack. Both the Chinese and Greek also used bees. They figured out how to <u>catapult</u> all kinds of objects. They would catapult stones and boiling oil over fortress walls. The Romans learned how to catapult a beehive. They would use these bee bombs on enemy ships that they feared would attack.

Bee bombs were still used even in World War I and World War II. Today, scientists are trying to figure out new ways to use bees for attacks.

In the first paragraph, the word <u>ancient</u> is a synonym for ____.

   A   very old

   B   very new

   C   modern

   D   common

> <u>Ancient</u> is a word used in social studies to describe people that lived a very long time ago. The best synonym would be "very old." The correct answer is choice A. "Modern" and "very new" do not describe something that is old. "Common" describes how often something appears or is used.

In the first paragraph, the word <u>dummy</u> means ____.

   A   pot

   B   real

   C   fake

   D   weapon

> A <u>dummy</u> is a fake body or object. The Mayans made a fake person, or dummy. The correct answer is choice C. A <u>dummy</u> is not a pot, real, or a weapon.

In paragraph 2, the word <u>fortress</u> means _____.

A a protected place

B a round building

C a tall building

D an open field

A <u>fortress</u> can be any shape or height. However, it must be a place that offers protection to the people inside. The correct answer is choice A. Choices B, C, and D are incorrect.

In paragraph 3, the word <u>catapult</u> is used as a verb. Describe the action of a <u>catapult</u>.

The word <u>catapult</u> can be used as both a verb and a noun. A <u>catapult</u> was used as weapon by ancient warriors. Here is a sample answer:

A <u>catapult</u> flings or throws objects through the air.

Read the passage. Then answer the questions.

Black-Footed Ferrets

Many people keep ferrets as pets. They are soft, easy to train, and playful. There are many types of ferrets, and many still live in the wild. There is one specific ferret that had not been seen since 1937. This is the black-footed ferret. The last time someone saw this kind of ferret was on a Canadian <u>prairie</u>. Scientists thought this ferret was <u>extinct</u>.

Yet, in 1981, scientists found a very small group of black-footed ferrets in Wyoming. This was an important <u>discovery</u>. Scientists wanted to increase the <u>population</u> of these ferrets. They believed the best way to do this was to keep them <u>protected</u> in zoos.

This plan worked well. There are now more than 300 black-footed ferrets in zoos. Many black-footed ferrets have been <u>released</u> into the wild. There will be many more released back into the grasslands in the coming years.

In the first paragraph, the word prairie is a synonym for ____.

A zoo

C wetlands

B desert

D grasslands

✓ Prairie is a science word. If you look at the last paragraph, you will see that the word *grasslands* is used. This gives you a clue that a prairie has something to do with grasslands. A prairie is not a zoo, desert, or wetland. Choices A, B, and C are incorrect. The correct answer is choice D.

In the first paragraph, the word extinct means ____.

A busy

C gone forever

B active

D here to stay

✓ You may not know what the word extinct means. Yet, as you read the rest of the article, you begin to understand its meaning. Scientists were worried that the ferrets would be gone forever. The correct answer is choice C. Something that is extinct is gone forever. It is not not mean busy, active, or here to stay.

Write definitions for the other underlined words in the passage. If you can't tell the meaning of the word from the context, look it up in a print or online dictionary.

discovery _____

population _____

protected _____

released _____

✓ Did you get them all? Your answers might read something like these:

discovery—finding something
population—count of how many exist
protected—kept safe
released—out on the loose

Test Yourself

The Tale of Cupid and Psyche

a retelling of a Roman myth

There was once a king and queen who had three daughters. The youngest was named Psyche. She was so beautiful that all humans <u>adored</u> her. Soon they stopped praying to Venus, the goddess of beauty.

Psyche was very beautiful, but nobody wanted to marry her. Her parents were concerned about this and went to an <u>oracle</u>. This priestess told them that Psyche was <u>destined</u> to marry a monster. The oracle told them to take Psyche to a faraway rock and leave her there.

The goddess Venus had become extremely envious of Psyche. She sent her son Cupid down to the human world. He carried his bow and arrow and <u>vials</u> of poison. The poison would make Psyche fall in love with a monster.

Cupid made himself invisible. Then he flew down to Psyche sleeping on a rock. When he saw her beautiful face, he was so <u>enamored</u> that he dropped his arrow. Cupid pricked himself with the arrow meant for her. He fell in love with her himself.

Soon Psyche awoke on her rock but she didn't find a monster. Instead, she found a loving but invisible husband. Cupid told Psyche that she would never marry a monster. Instead, they would live together if she believed in his love for her. He told her he would visit her by night. However, she must never try to see him during the day. She agreed, and they went to live in a beautiful palace.

She missed her family very much. Psyche begged Cupid to let her sisters visit her. He agreed. Her sisters were jealous of the way that Psyche lived. They put doubts and fears in her head about her husband. They told her that she had married a monster and that she must discover what he looked like.

Psyche was so upset by this that she went to Venus and begged to know the truth. Venus set up a series of tests for Psyche, all of which she passed. Still jealous, Venus put Psyche into a deep sleep. Finally, Cupid begged the god Jupiter to put an end to the fighting between Venus and Psyche. He asked Jupiter to unite him with Psyche. Jupiter then made Psyche a goddess. Cupid and Psyche were then united forever.

1 In the first paragraph, the word <u>adored</u> is a synonym for ____.

 A hated

 B prized

 C enjoyed

 D unloved

2 In paragraph 2, the word <u>oracle</u> means ____.

 A human

 B monster

 C priestess

 D god

3 As used in paragraph 2, <u>destined</u> means ____.

 A fated

 B history

 C presented

 D lucked out

4 A <u>vial</u> is ____.

 A a ship

 B an arrow

 C a large glass jug

 D a small glass bottle

UNIT 1 ✖✖✖✖✖✖✖✖✖✖✖✖✖✖✖✖✖✖✖✖✖✖✖✖✖✖✖✖✖✖✖✖✖✖✖✖
Vocabulary Development

5 In paragraph 4, the word <u>enamored</u> is a synonym for _____.

    A liked

    B hated

    C disliked

    D fell in love

6 Explain the origins of the word <u>cupid</u> and its relationship to the myth of Cupid and Psyche.

_____

_____

_____

_____

_____

7 How are the words <u>Venus</u> and <u>Jupiter</u> used in science?

_____

_____

_____

_____

_____

REVIEW

Vocabulary Development

Read the passage. Then answer the questions.

Secret Language

by Hope Beauvais

Every day I see Maya and Shannon making hand <u>gestures</u> to each other. They have their own secret language, just like a couple of meowing cats. I don't like it, and I want to be part of their club. It's not fair!

Today in gym class, Maya and Shannon were making hand gestures again. We were playing basketball, and Maya was supposed to be on my team. We were winning. But Maya tossed the ball to Shannon. She even used the hand gesture to "run." Our teams tied.

In the school bus line after school today, I was so busy <u>studying</u> Shannon and Maya as they talked to each other in their own language that I almost missed my bus.

When I got home, I talked to my mother about Maya and Shannon. I told her how I wanted to be friends with them. However, they have their own secret language and they don't share it with anyone else.

My mom had the phone list for all the kids in school. She <u>resolved</u> to call Maya's mother, but nobody answered. Then she called Shannon's mom. Shannon's dad answered.

I listened to every word that I could, as <u>little pitchers have big ears</u>. I heard something about Shannon's mom needing to use this secret language to <u>communicate</u> with Shannon. That's strange!

When she finished talking to Shannon's dad, my mom explained everything. "Shannon and Maya have something in common," she said.

"Yes, their secret language!" I said.

"Yes, but—" my mom paused. "They need to use this secret language to communicate with their mothers. They are using sign language. Both of their mothers are deaf."

"You mean, Shannon's mom and Maya's mom can't hear anything?" I said.

"Yes. They have always been deaf, and have never experienced the sounds that you and I have always heard," my mom explained sadly. "They have never heard the wind *whoosh* through the leaves. They have never heard the *buzz* of a bee. They have never heard the sounds we take for granted."

"Well, that's just not fair!" I said, and the phrase had a whole new meaning.

1 Which of these words is a synonym for <u>gestures</u>?

A hands

B silent

C movements

D unmoving

2 Read this sentence from the passage.

In the school bus line after school today, I was so busy studying Shannon and Maya talking to each other in their own language that I almost missed my bus.

Which of these is an antonym for <u>studying</u> as it is used in the sentence?

A noticing

B looking at

C ignoring

D taking it in

3 Which *best* fits the meaning of <u>resolved</u> as it is used in paragraph 5?

A decided

B solved

C separated

D repeat

4 The word <u>communicate</u> in paragraph 6 means _____.

   A a way to share writing

   B a way to share thoughts

   C speaking only with words

   D speaking only with hands

5 In paragraph 1, what simile does the author use to describe the secret language the two girls are using?

_____

_____

_____

_____

6 Explain the meaning of the idiom <u>little pitchers have big ears</u> in paragraph 6.

_____

_____

_____

_____

UNIT 1 ❌❌❌❌❌❌❌❌❌❌❌❌❌❌❌❌❌❌❌❌❌❌❌
Vocabulary Development

Odysseus

by Giovanni Thomas

Odysseus was a great leader of ancient Greece. He was a hero during the Trojan War, but after the war it took him 10 years of sailing, his Odyssey, *to return home to his wife and son.*

Shall we go on an Odyssey—
To become the heroes we were meant to be?
Shall we go on a quest—
And learn what can be our personal best?

5 Shall we take a ship to sea—
To find out the hero we were meant to be?
Shall we sit and stew in grief—
Or shall we stand up for something we believe?

Life, like a buffet of food, gives us many choices.
10 How will you balance all your desires?
Life is a beautiful garden which can calm us.
How will you know when to choose and when?

7 In line 9, what is being compared in the simile?

A life and food

B giving and food

C life and many choices

D giving and many choices

8 Explain the metaphor in line 11.

_____

_____

_____

_____

_____

9 From your understanding of the poem, what is an <u>odyssey</u>?

_____

_____

_____

_____

_____

Read the passage. Then answer the questions.

Energy

You might already know about solar power. This is using energy from the sun. You might even know about wind power that makes energy from wind. But have you ever heard of human power?

Think of a world of energy made by humans! People have <u>energy to burn</u>. They like to be active. People who have active lives are happy. Scientists are using this energy in different ways.

A new type of dance floor at a club in Europe uses human energy. As people dance, they pound their feet over and over. The floor takes in the energy. This makes enough electricity to run the light show.

Some new gyms are letting people listen to music that they power. People run on a treadmill. The people are making a type of energy by running in one place. A human-powered treadmill works like a windmill. The energy that the human-powered treadmills create runs the fans in the gym. This is how the gym stays cool without electricity. Some gym bicycles and treadmills let you power your own music!

Some animals produce extra energy. The electric eel is one of these. People are trying to use this energy. Eels have even been used to power holiday lights.

<u>Anything is possible if we put our minds to it.</u> We can learn to use what we have in the future. Our own energy can help give us the electricity we need.

10 What is <u>solar power</u>?

    A energy from the sun

    B energy from the moon

    C energy from humans

    D energy from the wind

11 *Electra* was a Greek mythological character. She was the goddess of storms and lightning. Explain which word (or words) from the passage is related to her.

_____

_____

_____

_____

12 Explain why the author uses the idiom <u>energy to burn</u> to describe humans.

_____

_____

_____

_____

13 What does the adage <u>anything is possible if we put our minds to it</u> mean?

_____

_____

_____

_____

_____

14 In the context of this passage, what is <u>human power</u>?

_____

_____

_____

_____

_____

UNIT 1 ▨▨▨▨▨▨▨▨▨▨▨▨▨▨▨▨▨▨▨▨▨▨▨▨▨▨▨▨▨▨▨
Vocabulary Development

Key Ideas and Details

Reading materials are all around you! You can find books that have stories, poems, and plays. You read, and you find out about the things you like. Everything you read has ideas and details.

This unit is about those ideas and details. As you read, you need to understand bigger ideas and smaller details. You need to know which details are important. And you need to know how they relate to one another.

- **In Lesson 4,** you'll learn how to recall details. Recalling details will help you remember what a text is about. You'll learn how to pick out details. Then you will learn how to join these details with others.

- **Lesson 5** is about bigger ideas the details support. You'll learn how to find the main idea of a text. Understanding the main idea will help you answer, "What's that reading about?" You'll know how the details support the main idea. Lastly, you'll learn how to summarize a text. That is, you will learn how to tell about the most important ideas and details.

- **Lesson 6** is about the relationship between the ideas and details. You'll learn about what makes up stories and plays. You'll learn how to find key details about the characters, events, and settings in a text. Then you will learn how they are connected with one another to tell a story.

- **Lesson 7** is about how ideas and details connect in nonfiction. People, events, and ideas relate to one another. These relationships help you understand the topic. You'll learn how to use them. Then you can better understand what you're reading.

Understanding a Text

RL.4.1, RI.4.1

Vocabulary
editor
invading
work camp

What makes a book fun to read? You may have noticed that a good book is full of details. Details make a book more enjoyable to read. The details an author uses in the text gives you important information. As you read, you should focus on **noting and recalling details.** If you don't understand the details, you will miss much of what the author is saying. Next time you read a book or article, see how many details you know when you finish.

Guided Practice

Read the passage. Then answer the questions.

Judy Blume was born on February 12, 1938, in Elizabeth, New Jersey. Her father was a dentist. Her mother was a stay-at-home mom. Judy's mom taught her to love books.

Judy often went to the library growing up. Judy read many books there. She had a lovely imagination. Judy was always making up stories in her head! No matter if she was running around outside or playing quietly inside, she was making up new stories. However, she never wrote down her stories. This early storytelling would help Judy become the author we know today.

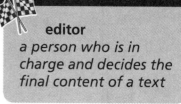

editor
a person who is in charge and decides the final content of a text

As a high school student, Judy was an editor for her school's newspaper. After high school, she studied education at New York University (NYU). There she met her husband. They had two children. While she stayed at home with them, she still wanted to be creative. Judy wanted to write, so she took classes at NYU. It was then that her career took off. She published her first book, *The One in the Middle is the Green Kangaroo,* in 1969.

In 1970, Judy wrote *Are You There, God? It's Me, Margaret.* This book was written for teens. Judy was recognized for writing about real events that teens face. Her next book, *Tales of a Fourth-Grade Nothing,* was published in 1972 and was the first in a series of five books. In this book, Judy tells of Peter's life with his younger brother Fudge. A book like this makes children laugh and want to read more!

Judy writes about what she knows. That is why her books take place in the cities where she has lived. She has sold more than 80 million books in 31 different languages.

Some of her other books include *Freckle Juice, Superfudge, Blubber,* and *Iggie's House.* Judy is still writing for people of all ages and working to turn her books into movies. She lives in Key West, Florida, with her husband.

Find a list of the books Judy Blume has written on the Internet. Make a tally of how many students in your class have read each book. Which book is the most popular?

Identify where Judy Blume grew up.

A   in Elizabeth, New Jersey

B   in Key West, Florida

C   at her high school

D   at NYU

Did you pay attention to the details? All of these places played a role in Judy's life. A key detail about where she was born tells you where Judy spent her early years. The first paragraph tells you directly that it wasn't in Florida, at NYU, or at her high school. Choice A is the correct answer.

Who first taught Judy to love books?

A   a librarian

B   her husband

C   her mother

D   her fourth-grade teacher

Details are important because they give you information. You can guess that the person who taught Judy to enjoy books is someone she will never forget. The last sentence of the first paragraph tells you that you can give credit not to her librarian, husband, or fourth-grade teacher, but her mother. Choice C is the correct answer.

Explain where Judy gets her ideas for her stories.

_____

_____

 We know that Judy Blume has always had a great imagination. She also read many books as a child. But every writer writes about what she knows. Paragraph 5 gives us the answer. Here is a sample answer:

Judy gets her ideas from her life and what she knows. That is why her books take place in the cities where she has lived.

Determine in which section of the library you would find Judy Blume's books.

A biography

B fiction

C reference

D history

 You know the answer to this question even though none of these words appears in the passage. The question asks you to **make an inference.** This means to join details that you read with details that you already know. Then you can find information that is not directly stated. Judy Blume writes stories about characters that are made up. You know that is fiction. History, reference books, and biographies all include facts. Choice B is the correct answer.

Explain why Judy took classes at NYU.

_____

_____

_____

 This is another question that you have to answer by inference. Paragraph 3 tells us, "While she stayed at home with them, she still wanted to be creative. Judy wanted to write, so she took classes at NYU." Here is a sample answer:

Judy wanted to be creative and write while she was home with her children, so she took writing classes to help her learn to be a better writer.

Now, note details in the first part of a story.

A Difficult Decision

by Stacy Rummel

I held my breath as Mrs. Hill passed back our math
tests. I did not get the chance to study for this test because
I had a soccer game. I promised my mom and dad that
soccer wouldn't get in the way of school. They want me to
get into the new middle school advanced program next
year, and I need to have good grades.

My heart raced as Mrs. Hill came to speak to me.

"Raul, this is not your best work," she said. "Let me
know if you need help."

I got a D? I said to myself. *Great!* I thought. *What am
I going to tell my mom and dad?*

"If you received a grade lower than a C on your test, please fix your
test for homework tonight," Mrs. Hill said.

When the bell rang at the end of the day, I ran out of the room. I
just wanted the day to be over. What was I going to tell my mom?

I could tell her I didn't get the test back. I could tell her I got a B.
That would be better than a D! But that would mean I would have
to lie. My mom and dad always told me to tell the truth. They said
children that tell the truth do the right thing. My mom and dad trusted
me. I didn't want that to change. I knew what I had to do.

I pushed open the back door.

"Hi, Raul! In the kitchen," Mom yelled. "How was your day?"

"Bad," I said as I sat down.

"Why?" Mom asked.

"Well, I got my math test back," I said.

"And?" Mom looked at me.

"I got a D. I have to do it for homework tonight," I said.

"Is soccer too much?" Mom asked.

"No!" I cried. "I'll do better on the next test!"

"We told you that you can only play soccer if you did well in school,"
Mom reminded me. "We want you to do the best you can in every class."

"I know I let you down. I wanted to lie, but you taught me to tell the truth," I said.

My mom looked at me. She came over and gave me a hug.

"Thank you," Mom said. "Let's look at that test and see what you did. I can help you fix it. I want to make sure you know what you did wrong so you can do better on the next one.

"Thanks, Mom! You are great!" I smiled.

Determine who the narrator is in the story.

A Mrs. Hill

B Mom

C Dad

D Raul

In this story, the narrator is one of the characters. You can tell that the narrator isn't Mrs. Hill, Mom, or Dad because the narrator refers to them by name. In paragraph 3, Mrs. Hill says, "Raul, this is not your best work." We know the narrator is Raul because he uses the first-person pronoun *I*. The correct answer is choice D.

Why do Raul's mom and dad want him to do well at school?

A He needs good grades for the middle school advanced program.

B He gets paid to earn good grades.

C His coach will make him stop playing soccer.

D He is failing his classes.

The story begins with Raul explaining that he was not able to study for a test and why he needed to do well on it. *Why* is an important detail of the story. Nowhere does Raul say he gets paid for good grades. He does not say that he is failing. Raul also does not say that his coach would make him quit soccer. Choices B, C, and D are incorrect. You learn in the first paragraph that Raul needs good grades to get into the new middle school advanced program. You can infer that choice A is the correct answer.

Determine which of these is *not* a detail that describes Raul.

A He plays soccer.

B He is truthful.

C He has brown eyes.

D He is in Mrs. Hill's class.

The passage tells us that Raul plays soccer, is truthful, and has Mrs. Hill for a teacher. One detail about Raul we do not know is the color of his eyes. Choice C is the correct answer.

What can you infer about Raul's age?

_____

This is another detail that helps you understand Raul. The passage does not say how old Raul is, so you have to infer this. Raul tells you that his mom and dad want him to get into the new middle school advanced program next year. Here is a sample answer:

Raul is in fifth or sixth grade, or about 10 or 11 years old.

Describe what Raul's mom is like. What is a detail in the story that gives you a clue?

_____

Think about what Raul's mother does in the story. She gave him a hug, and asked to look at the test to see what he did wrong so she could help him fix it. She also encouraged him to do better on the next test. Here is a sample answer:

Raul's mom is kind, loves him, and wants him to do well at school.

Test Yourself

Anne Frank

Anne Frank was born on June 12, 1929, in Frankfurt, Germany. She had an older sister, Margot. Like many lands, Germany had its problems. However, life in Germany became unbearable for some people after Adolf Hitler became its leader in 1933. Hitler was against anyone who had beliefs that were different from his. He was especially against the Jewish people living in the land. Anne's family was Jewish, and her parents were scared. They began to think about moving.

In 1933, the Franks moved to Amsterdam in Holland, part of the Netherlands. Her father established a business there. Anne and her sister started school. Even when Anne was young, she was confused. She always asked, "Why?"

World War II began when Hitler began invading other countries. The German army attacked the Netherlands in 1940. The Dutch army gave in. The German army took over the country where the Franks now lived. Hitler became more powerful.

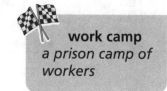

invading
entering another country with the purpose of taking it over

Hitler started making lists of anyone who was Jewish. In 1941, people had to tell the German army if they were Jewish. Their names were put on a list. Anne had to go to a special school for Jewish children. They were not allowed to go to the swimming pool, ride on the train, or go to the movie theater. By 1942, all Jewish people had to wear a yellow star on their shirt that said "Jew." It told others who they were.

Anne received a diary as a gift from her parents in June 1942. She began writing in it. She listed the many things her family could not do because they were Jewish. The list grew longer.

Anne's family said it was time to hide. It had become even more unsafe to be Jewish with the Germans in charge of the country. Many Jews were being sent to jails and work camps. The Franks packed the things they would really need. They hid in a space in her father's office building. His four workers helped by bringing them food and books. Anne wrote about what was happening in her diary. She wrote, "The nicest part is being able to write down all my thoughts and feelings…."

work camp
a prison camp of workers

In 1944, Anne and her family were discovered in their hiding place. All were taken to a work camp. Everyone but Anne's father died in the camps. When her father returned to Amsterdam, he was given Anne's diary. He made sure it was published. It became *Anne Frank: The Diary of a Young Girl.* The diary tells of her strength during a very difficult time in her life. It gives readers an idea of what her life was like as a Jew during World War II.

1 Anne Frank was born in _____.

   A Amsterdam

   B the Netherlands

   C the United States

   D Germany

2 Anne's story takes place during _____.

   A the 1930s and 1940s

   B World War I

   C the early 20th century

   D the U.S. Civil War

3 Who was Margot?

   A Anne's best friend

   B a neighbor

   C Anne's sister

   D Anne's mother

4 Jewish people stood out from other people because they _____.

   A drove special cars

   B wore a yellow star

   C were put in schools

   D had to live on trains

5 Why were Jewish people so scared before and during World War II?
Use details from the passage to answer this question.

_____

_____

_____

_____

_____

6 Explain why you think Anne wrote about what was happening.

_____

_____

_____

_____

Main Idea and Summaries

RL.4.2, RI.4.2

Vocabulary
battery
exploration
nonrenewable
parched
renewable
wayfarers

Your friend wants to tell you about a book he's just read. Your first question is probably, "What's it about?" If he really understood the book, he can tell you what it was about in one sentence.

Every bit of text you read is *about* something. Every text has a main idea. Stating the **main idea** means you will answer the question, "What's it about?" Being able to answer this question is an important reading skill. When you know what you are reading *about,* details make sense. The main ideas of a section of text are the details that support the main ideas of the whole section.

Guided Practice

Read the passage. Then answer the questions.

Seaman Saves the Day

exploration
the act of traveling to discover more about a new place

When Lewis and Clark set off to explore the American West, a furry, four-legged friend joined them. This furry friend named Seaman was Lewis's Newfoundland dog. Seaman was a well-known member of the team of explorers. Lewis bought Seaman for $20 in 1803. He wrote about Seaman in his journal. Because Lewis's handwriting was hard to read, people thought the dog's name was "Scannon."

Lewis's dog saved their Native American guide, Sacagawea, and the men from being killed many times. One night, a bear came near their camp. Seaman saw the bear and barked at it. The men heard the barking and came out and shot the bear before it could hurt any of them.

Another time, Seaman saw a large buffalo bull that had come near their tent. He made the buffalo move away just by being there. Lewis wrote, "When he came near the tent, my dog saved us by causing him to change his course." Seaman protected the camp from many dangerous animals.

As a hunter, Seaman helped catch food for the explorers. Seaman once found a deer that was drinking water at a river. Seaman charged it and the deer became food for the very hungry team. He saved their lives by helping them find food to eat.

Seaman became an important member of the exploration team. We imagine him riding in their boat and running along side them as they traveled. He was always watching for animals that could hurt them. His bark would tell them that something was wrong.

Without Seaman, the team would have experienced many more dangers on their trip west! Perhaps we would not know the West as we know it now without Seaman.

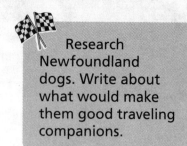
Research Newfoundland dogs. Write about what would make them good traveling companions.

What is this article *mainly* about?

A the American West

B Lewis and Clark's travels

C Sacagawea

D Seaman

The passage is "about" all these things in some way. The "American West," "Lewis and Clark's travels," and "Sacagawea" are mentioned in the article but they are not what the passage is mainly about. The passage is mostly about Seaman. Choice D is the correct answer.

Which sentence *best* expresses the main idea of the first paragraph?

A When Lewis and Clark set off to explore the American West, a furry, four-legged friend joined them.

B This furry friend named Seaman was Lewis's Newfoundland dog.

C Lewis bought Seaman for $20 in 1803.

D Because Lewis's handwriting was hard to read, people thought the dog's name was "Scannon."

In most paragraphs, there is one sentence that tells the main idea of the paragraph. It's called the **topic sentence**. In this paragraph, the first sentence is the topic sentence: "When Lewis and Clark set off to explore the American West, a furry, four-legged friend joined them." The sentences that follow give more details about the topic. Choice A is the correct answer.

62

UNIT 2 ▪▪
Key Ideas and Details

Identify the topic sentence of the second paragraph.

This paragraph tells readers how Seaman protected Sacagawea and the men from dangerous animals. Details that support this topic include how Seaman saved them from a bear that came into their camp. The answer is a restatement of the first sentence:

Seaman protected the camp from many dangerous animals.

Identify the topic sentence of the fourth paragraph.

The first and last sentences tell of Seaman's ability to catch animals that the team would eat. He provided food so that the explorers could stay alive. The sentences in the middle of the paragraph support the main idea by telling more information about how Seaman caught a deer. Here is a sample answer:

Seaman helped the team stay alive by catching food for them to eat.

Determine which of these ideas should be left out of a summary of the passage.

A As a hunter, Seaman helped catch food for the explorers.

B Seaman was a well-known member of the team of explorers.

C Because Lewis's handwriting was hard to read, people thought the dog's name was "Scannon."

D Seaman protected the camp from many dangerous animals.

A **summary** is a retelling of the main ideas and important details in a passage. For this passage, choices A, B, and D are all important details. A summary of the passage doesn't need to give a specific detail that people thought Seaman's name was "Scannon." The correct answer is choice B.

Write a summary of the passage.

_____

_____

_____

_____

_____

 You can summarize a passage by thinking of the main ideas of each section or paragraph. Here is a sample answer:

Seaman is Lewis's dog that accompanied him, Clark, Sacagawea, and the rest of the explorers as they traveled through the American West. Seaman protected the camp from large animals, caught animals for them to eat as food, and helped them stay alive. Seaman was an important member of the exploration team.

Read the passage. Then answer the questions.

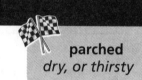
parched
dry, or thirsty

The Talkative Tortoise

a fable from India

Tortoise lived near a pond in the enormous forest. One beautiful day, he spotted two geese that had come to the pond for a drink.

"Why haven't we seen you here before?" the geese asked Tortoise.

"Well, I usually stay indoors," Tortoise said. "I prefer to be alone because I don't have many friends."

"We hope to see you again," the geese said as they departed.

Tortoise began to leave his home more, and he often met the geese at the pond. They all had fun together.

Soon, the pond started to dry up. The animals had a difficult time finding food. Before the geese left to find a new place to live, they visited Tortoise.

"We have decided it is time to move before we die in this desertlike forest. The pond has nearly dried up," the geese told Tortoise. "We hope you have a prosperous life, and we will surely miss you."

 UNIT 2
Key Ideas and Details
64

"Don't leave me behind to become parched and die!" Tortoise yelled. "Please take me with you; I beg you!"

"How can birds that fly take a tortoise that travels on the ground? You can't fly!" they said to Tortoise.

"I know, but I have a plan. I will explain how you can take me with you if you promise you won't leave me," Tortoise said.

"If we can take you, we will. What is your suggestion?" they asked Tortoise.

Tortoise told the geese that he would find a sturdy stick. The two geese would each hold one end of the stick in their beaks as they flew. Tortoise would use his mouth to hold onto the middle of the stick while they flew. The geese would be able to carry him to their new dwelling place.

"We think that will work," one of the geese said. "Let's go search for a stick!"

Before they began to soar, the geese reminded Tortoise that while they were flying and he was holding on to the stick, he would not be able to move his mouth. He wouldn't be able to utter a sound.

"You must not talk while we are flying. If you do, your mouth will open and you will plummet toward the earth and surely die," they said. "Please stay absolutely quiet until we find a new pond."

"I am not ignorant," the Tortoise said. "I know what will happen if I mutter a sound."

Tortoise enjoyed seeing the beautiful sights on the journey. However, when they came to a large city, he heard people shouting about two geese carrying a silly tortoise. Tortoise could see that they were pointing at him. They were laughing at him so much that he wanted to hide in his shell. He didn't like that they were saying hurtful things about him, and he became angry.

When he couldn't take it any more, Tortoise opened his mouth to yell back at the people. He fell from the sky and landed on the ground near the crowd.

"What a stupid tortoise," the people said while the geese cried that they lost their friend.

"Didn't Tortoise know that happiness comes from keeping quiet?" the geese asked each other.

What makes the geese decide they need to leave the forest?

A The geese were bored.

B The pond is nearly dry.

C Tortoise is annoying the geese.

D The geese wanted to fly south.

This question asks about a detail that supports the main idea of the story. The story does not say that the geese were bored or that Tortoise is annoying the geese. And it does not say that that the geese wanted to fly south. The story does say that the forest has become like a desert and the pond is drying up. The correct answer is choice B.

How does Tortoise respond when the geese tell him not to talk while they are traveling?

A He laughs at them.

B He refuses to go with them because he is afraid.

C He tells them he understands this and is not stupid.

D He finds another way to travel to the new pond.

This is another detail that supports the main idea. Tortoise can't believe the geese would think he is so stupid that he would open his mouth to talk while they are flying. He tells them he knows better than to let go of the stick while they are in the air. He does not laugh or refuse to go with them. Tortoise does not find another way to travel. Choice C is the correct answer.

What is the main idea of this story?

The main idea of a text is sometimes called its **theme**. The theme is different from the plot. The plot tells what happens. The theme is what a text is about. In a fable, the theme is often told as a lesson, or "moral." The lesson results from the way the main character responds to challenges. Tortoise is made a fool because he can't believe the geese remind him to hold onto the stick. He tells them that nothing would be so important that he would open his mouth to speak. Yet, when people laugh at him, he becomes too angry to keep quiet. Here is a sample answer:

The main idea is "Happiness comes from keeping quiet."

Determine which sentence *best* summarizes how Tortoise would travel.

A He would hold onto the middle of a large stick while the geese carry him and the stick through the air.

B One of the geese would carry a stick while Tortoise held on to it.

C Tortoise would follow the geese by swimming to their new home in a distant pond.

D The geese would hold a stick between them while tortoise held on and floated on the water behind them.

Choice A best summarizes how Tortoise would travel to his new home with the geese because it gives the most detailed summary. Tortoise held onto the middle of a sturdy stick while the geese each held one end of the stick in their beaks. Then the threesome flew to their new home. More than one of the geese held the stick. Tortoise did not swim to the new pond. He also did not float behind the geese.

Write a summary of the story.

_____

_____

_____

_____

_____

_____

_____

_____

 Because the story is short, your summary should be even shorter. Your answer should include only the main things that happen in the story. Here is a sample answer:

Tortoise doesn't want to stay in the forest because the pond is drying up and his friends, the geese, are leaving. He tells the geese that he wants to go come with them. He says that if they each carry one end of a stick, then he can hold on to the middle while they fly. The geese agree and remind him not to talk while they are flying. Tortoise laughs that they would remind him not to talk. However, when people start to laugh at Tortoise when they see him flying, he becomes angry and opens his mouth to yell at them. Then he falls to the ground.

Uphill

by Christina Rosetti

Does the road wind uphill all the way?
Yes, to the very end.
Will the day's journey take the whole long day?
From morn to night, my friend.

5 But is there for the night a resting-place?
A roof for when the slow, dark hours begin.
May not the darkness hide it from my face?
You cannot miss that inn.

Shall I meet other wayfarers[1] at night?
10 Those who have gone before.
Then must I knock, or call when just in sight?
They will not keep you waiting at that door.

Shall I find comfort, travel-sore and weak?
Of labor you shall find the sum.
15 Will there be beds for me and all who seek?
Yea, beds for all who come.

What is the main idea that Rosetti expresses in this poem?

    A   When we travel to any place, we always go uphill.

    B   Life's travels are hard, but you find friends and rest.

    C   We will all find a place to rest on a bed during life's journey.

    D   People will wait for you, and they will give you a bed to rest.

Rosetti was an important female poet in England in the 1800s. She was brought up in a family of poets and artists. She was religious. Many of her poems reflect that. In "Uphill," Rosetti compares walking up a hill to a journey through life. Look at the first line of each stanza. Each is a question and main idea for the stanza. Choices A, C, and D are not the main theme. The theme is expressed by choice B, the correct answer.

[1]**wayfarers:** people who travel on foot

Interpret what Rosetti means by "Will there be beds for me and all who seek?" in line 15.

In this poem, Rosetti is asking questions about her journey through life. The journey is not easy and is filled will difficulty. In each stanza, she crafts the main idea as a question. Then she uses details to answer her question. In the last stanza, she asks about the final resting place. Look to the lines that follow the question to answer the question above. Here is a sample answer:

Rosetti is saying that at the end of our lives we will find rest.

UNIT 2 ▓▓
Key Ideas and Details

Test Yourself

Battery Power for Your House

Is it possible for a battery to power a whole house? It is no longer a dream, but something that could happen soon. Then we would no longer depend on oil for our power. We would also use more clean energy that would help our world.

One company has been working to create such a battery. After ten years of work, Ceramatec has built a battery that could change the way we use power in our homes. This new battery stores power from the sun. It is called a deep-storage battery. Today, we get our electricity from a power grid. This grid is very old. It depends on fossil fuels to create the power we need. We would pull much less energy from the power grid by using this new battery.

This battery has enough power to run all the appliances and machines in our homes. It would provide power for more than four hours. It can be recharged 3,560 times every day and will last for ten years. It would cost about $2,000, or 3 cents per kilowatt-hour. This costs less than the power we use today. Electricity from the power grid costs 8 cents per kilowatt-hour. This battery would really help people save money!

Not only would this battery help us save money, but it is also safe. Batteries are not used inside our homes today because they are too hot and powerful. They are also filled with a liquid. This liquid is poisonous. These new batteries are made of a solid. They can store large amounts of energy, but they do not get hot.

Would we recharge the batteries using the power grid? No! These batteries use solar or wind power. At the end of the day, we would plug them into a solar panel or windmill. We would not need to use the old power grid. This grid uses energy from nonrenewable sources like oil. These new batteries would be a clean energy source. They use renewable energy from the sun or wind.

Ceramatec is working hard to make their batteries available soon.

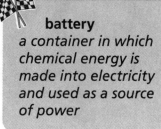

battery
a container in which chemical energy is made into electricity and used as a source of power

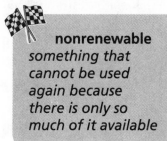

renewable
something that can be used or renewed again because there is plenty of it

nonrenewable
something that cannot be used again because there is only so much of it available

1 What is the main idea of this article?

   A Deep-storage batteries would save money.

   B A new rechargable battery can power your house.

   C Ceramatec's battery is powered by clean energy sources.

   D Deep-storage batteries are safe.

2 What is the *most* important supporting idea of this article?

   A Deep-storage batteries would be a clean way to replace our old power grid.

   B Other powerful batteries are too hot and dangerous to have in our homes.

   C Yesterday's science fiction can become today's technology.

   D Deep-storage batteries would cost $2,000 and supply power for more than four hours.

3 Determine the main idea of paragraph 3.

   A This battery is small enough to fit in our house.

   B Electricity from the power grid costs 8 cents per kilowatt-hour.

   C The battery would help people save money.

   D It can be recharged 3,650 times a day for ten years.

4 Identify which of these would make the *best* heading for paragraph 4.

   A Made to Be Clean

   B No Need to Use the Grid

   C Powerful and Safe

   D Battery Facts and Figures

UNIT 2 ▓▓
Key Ideas and Details

5 Write a sentence that expresses the main idea of paragraph 5.

_____

_____

_____

_____

_____

6 Write a summary of the article.

_____

_____

_____

_____

_____

Literary Elements

RL.4.3

Vocabulary

dumb
exhilaration
ladybird
grenadier
scythe

What do you like about works of fiction? Is it the **characters** and how they talk to one another? Maybe it is the **plot,** the sequence of **events** that happened in the story. Maybe it is the **setting.** The setting is when and where the story takes place.

All these elements are in a good story. The characters and the ways they think, feel, and act help move the plot along. The setting helps form the characters and determines what they do.

A story may be realistic fiction, a myth or folktale, a fantasy, or a tale set in the past. It can even be told in a poem. However the story is told, it will always include characters, plot, and setting.

Analyzing a Character

Characters make the story real. An author usually describes how characters look, talk, and behave. The "talk" part is called **dialogue.** Sometimes the way a character talks can be as important as what he or she says. You can learn about characters in stories in several ways:

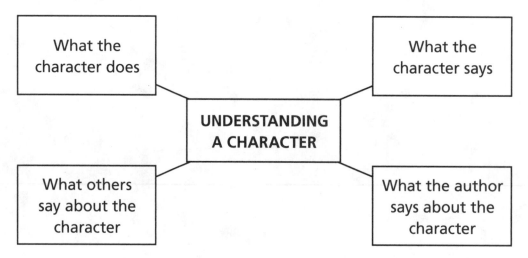

What the character does		What the character says
	UNDERSTANDING A CHARACTER	
What others say about the character		What the author says about the character

Guided Practice

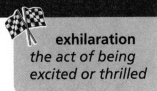

exhilaration
the act of being excited or thrilled

Race Man

I put my arm securely around Flash. He licks my nose and wags his tail.

"So long, ol' boy," I tell him, "I'm going to miss you."

He looks at me with ears raised expectantly. I can tell by the way his tail is thumping easily on my bed that he wants to accompany me.

"Sorry, buddy, but you're too enormous for the cockpit, and your hair would get all over everything," I apologize. "Anyway, mom and dad would miss you too much."

At the racetrack, the stands loom high above me and pit row is deserted except for me. It is absolutely quiet—much different than it is on race day when fans are yelling, waving flags, and cheering.

I lower my helmet onto my head, secure the strap, and flip down my visor. I slide through the window of my car and lower myself onto my seat. I turn the key and rev the engine as loud as it will go as sweat drips down the side of my face.

Pulling the harness over my body, I secure myself to the seat. I can see the track in front of me—it's hot and the sun is shining down on the black asphalt, heat radiating from it.

The rumble of the car gives me the motivation I need, and I push the accelerator all the way to the floor. Tires spinning, smoke billowing from them, I turn the wheel slightly, and I'm off, exiting pit row.

The track in front of me takes my mind off my horrible mood. In my car, I'm able to drive and forget about everything else around me. I concentrate on the exhilaration I feel racing at 200 miles an hour. I take the first turn easily, holding tightly to the wheel. As the car aligns for the straightaway, I am reminded of my favorite NASCAR driver.

"I bet he doesn't have rotten days like I do," I whisper to myself. "I bet his mom never bossed him around when he was my age."

"Kevin!" I hear my mom call my name. Hopping off my bed, I run down the hallway, almost knocking down my little sister on the way to the kitchen.

"What took you so long? I've called you three times!" Mom wonders.

"Ummm…I was just daydreaming," I reply.

"Matt is waiting for you in the driveway, and he'd like to shoot some hoops with you," Mom says.

"If I can play with Matt, why can't I play with Dan?" I ask my mom. "They are both older than me."

"Yes, they are both older than you, Kevin, but Matt is a delightful boy. I don't like how Dan speaks to other children in the neighborhood. When you are a parent, maybe you will understand," Mom explains to me.

I shake my head, as I have no other choice.

"I know you think I'm being mean, but you have to trust me," Mom says.

"I know," I sigh.

"The people we choose as friends now will help determine our character later in life. I have noticed that Dan is mean to the other children, and I don't want him influencing you. You are a great boy, you treat others as you want to be treated, and I want it to stay that way," Mom says.

"Okay, Mom," I say. "May I take some of those delicious cookies outside for us? I could smell them from my room."

"You sure can! Have fun!" Mom calls after me.

Identify which of the following *best* describes Kevin.

A mean

B shy

C treats others unfairly

D treats others well

We know from Kevin's mom that he is nice. She tells him that he "treats others as you want to be treated." From these phrases, we know that choice D is the correct answer. Kevin is not mean, shy, or unfair.

UNIT 2 ▓▓
Key Ideas and Details

Which of the following *best* describes Kevin's mom?

A unloving

B humorous

C concerned over friendships

D unaware of what's going on

We can understand more about Kevin's mom by thinking about what she says to him. At the end of this story, we know that Kevin is upset with her because she won't let him play with Dan. She tells Kevin, "The people we choose as friends now will help determine our character later in life." We know she isn't unaware of what's going on, unloving, or humorous at this moment. Choice C is the best answer.

Describe Kevin as the main character in the story, as well as the plot and setting.

_____

_____

_____

_____

_____

_____

_____

Here is a sample answer:

At the beginning of the story, Kevin is in his bedroom with his dog. We learn later in the story that the time he spends on the racetrack racing his car is a daydream. It makes him feel better because he is in a bad mood. He is brought back to the present when his mom calls him to tell him his friend is outside. We learn that Kevin is upset because his mom tells him he can't play with one of the boys in the neighborhood. She explains why she made this decision. Then Kevin goes outside to play basketball with Matt. The story takes place in Kevin's bedroom, at the imaginary racetrack, and in his kitchen.

Explain how you knew that Kevin wasn't really at the racetrack.

_____

_____

_____

_____

_____

 After reading more of the story, you realize Kevin was not at the racetrack. Here is a sample answer:

> We know Kevin still lives at home when he tells his dog he can't come with him because his mom and dad would miss him. We also learn that Kevin must have had an argument with his mom and that's why he is upset. Kevin is too young to drive a car. It seems like Kevin is dreaming about racing a car. Then Kevin tells his mom he was "daydreaming" when she called him.

Elements of Drama

Dramatic literature is written to be performed by actors. Like other forms of narrative, dramatic writing tells a story. It uses special features that give instructions to directors and performers to make the story exciting for the audience.

A **play** is a story that is performed by actors. A play is usually divided into **acts** and **scenes** just like a book is divided into chapters. A scene is part of the action that takes place in a setting.

A list of the **characters** is called the **cast.** They perform the play's action. The cast appears at the beginning of the play.

The **setting** is when and where the action happens. Sometimes, the setting is described to the audience by the narrator. Other times, you can tell the setting by the set up of the stage.

Dialogue is the lines, or words, that characters speak. In a **script,** or printed version of a play, dialogue follows the character's name.

Stage directions tell actors how to move around the stage and talk. In a script, the characters' names, dialogue, and stage directions are printed in different styles of type so that readers can easily spot each of them.

Props are objects that are used by the characters on a stage, such as a pad of paper or a bike. **Scenery** is the backgrounds and larger objects that create the setting of the play. **Lighting** refers to the types of lights used on stage and how bright they are. The props, scenery, and lighting are usually described in the stage directions.

Guided Practice

Read the play. Then answer the questions.

An Earth Day Celebration

CHARACTERS:

Bobby, 9 years old

Juan, 9 years old

Abby, 8 years old

Lilia, 8 years old

Mrs. Ruiz, a teacher

Scene 1

Mrs. Ruiz's fourth-grade classroom. The classroom includes desks, a computer station, a few tables, and a teacher's desk. The school day is over, but a few students still remain working in the classroom. Some of the lights in the classroom are turned off but the computers remain on. Mrs. Ruiz is sitting behind her desk grading papers.

JUAN *(staring intently at his computer screen and speaking to no one in particular):* Did you know that the first Earth Day was held in 1970?

ABBY *(looking up at Juan while she continues to work on a project at the table):* It's cool to think Earth Day has been celebrated for more than 40 years.

LILIA: We have to make this the best Earth Day parade ever! I want everyone who comes to get excited!

BOBBY *(looking up from his computer):* There are so many things we can do to help our planet. I want to make sure we show some of them in our parade.

JUAN: What were you thinking?

BOBBY *(scratching his head):* Well, one of us can carry a recycle bin with a rope around his neck—kind of like a drummer in a marching band.

LILIA: Abby and I are working on the posters and banners. We are using recycled paper and materials to make them.

ABBY: We are going to include facts on them, too.

MRS. RUIZ *(gets up from her chair and joins the students):* Abby, that is a wonderful idea. Can anyone think of a way to show others they should remember to turn off the lights when they leave the room?

JUAN: What about someone in the parade wearing a large light bulb cut out from poster board over his chest? And even better, with a lampshade on his head! *(Juan laughs to himself.)*

LILIA: Juan, since you came up with that idea, you can wear it! I am not wearing a lampshade on my head!

MRS. RUIZ *(shaking her head):* OK, OK students. That's a good idea, Juan. I'll expect you to do it yourself or find someone else who is willing.

ABBY *(with excitement):* I know! Some of the people in the parade can ride their bikes or scooters. That will remind people to ride their bikes instead of driving their cars when they can.

BOBBY: That's an awesome idea, Abby. Maybe I can get my little brother, Mikey, to ride his little car in the parade. We can make a big circle with a line through it to tape to the back of the car.

LILIA: We could carry reusable water bottles and hand out some of the water bottles the local stores donated to us.

MRS. RUIZ: Good idea, Lilia! We can't forget about all the donations. We can carry the reusable shopping bags and put some of the information packets we made in them.

ABBY: I've finished the packets and brochures.

MRS. RUIZ: It sounds like everything is under control for a successful Earth Day parade. I'm so thankful to you four for all your extra work on this project. Finish up so you can be ready when your parents arrive to pick you up.

Scene 2

The grassy front lawn of the school near the flagpole. Posters and banners are scattered about. Bobby, Lilia, Juan, and Mrs. Ruiz are busy putting finishing touches on the things needed for the parade.

BOBBY *(pulling a red wagon behind him):* Here's the wagon we can use to move the compost bin through the parade route. Abby is finishing the sign that attaches to the side of it.

JUAN *(looking at his watch):* Just to let you know, we have 15 minutes until the other fourth grade classes and our own classmates will be here to line up. Let's go everyone; we can do this!

LILIA *(looking frantic):* 15 minutes! No! We need to have more time than that!

MRS. RUIZ: I'm afraid not, my dear. You've worked hard for the past two weeks, and we are plenty ready.

ABBY *(putting her arm around Lilia):* Mrs. Ruiz is right. We have done much more than the fourth graders last year! This parade is gonna rock!

BOBBY *(pointing into the audience and waving):* Look, there's Mikey and my mom! It's show time, people!

Which of these sentences *best* describes the interaction between Mrs. Ruiz and her students?

A Mrs. Ruiz is mean and yells at the students.

B Mrs. Ruiz doesn't speak to her students very much.

C Mrs. Ruiz tries to ignore her students so they don't bother her.

D Mrs. Ruiz encourages and praises her students.

We can tell from the dialogue with her students that Mrs. Ruiz is not mean and does not yells at them (choice A). We know that she *does* ask them questions and speaks with them (choice B). She does not ignore her students (choice C). On many occasions, Mrs. Ruiz offers encouragement and praise. The correct answer is choice D.

Identify which of these lines from scene 2 is an example of dialogue spoken by Juan.

A JUAN:

B We need to have more time than that!

C *(looking frantic)*

D Let's go everyone; we can do this!

This question tests your understanding of how to read a play. You noticed that *italic* type is used for stage directions (choice C), regular type for dialogue (choices B and D), and CAPITALS for the names of characters that tell who is speaking the dialogue (choice A). Choice B is a line that Lilia speaks. Choice D is Juan's line. Choice D is the correct answer.

Read the lines of this excerpt.

ABBY *(with excitement):* I know! Some of the people in the parade can ride their bikes or scooters.

What do the stage directions in this line tell you?

A Abby speaks the line with excitement.

B Abby cries as she speaks.

C Abby speaks the line without expression.

D Abby rides her bike across the stage.

The stage directions tell the actor playing Abby how she should speak the line. They tell her that she says the line *with* expression, so choice C is incorrect. "With excitement" does not mean to cry (choice B) or to move across the stage (choice D). The correct answer is choice A. The stage directions say Abby should speak the line as though she is excited about her idea.

Identify two props used in this play.

_____

A prop is an object that is easily moved and used by an actor. You wouldn't consider furniture or costumes to be props, but there are quite a few in this excerpt. Here is a sample answer:

One prop used in this play is a wagon. Another is a watch.

Contrast the settings of the two scenes in this excerpt. How do they appear to an audience?

_____

_____

_____

_____

_____

_____

 Here is a sample answer:

> The first scene takes place in Mrs. Ruiz's classroom. There are the usual objects you would see in the classroom: student desks, a teacher's desk, tables, and a computer station. This scene takes place inside. Scene 2 takes place outside on the grassy lawn in front of the school near the flagpole. There are students making preparations for a parade. The setting includes banners, posters, and a wagon.

The Dumb Soldier

by Robert Louis Stevenson

When the grass was closely mown,
Walking on the lawn alone,
In the turf a hole I found
And hid a soldier underground.

5   Spring and daisies came apace;
Grasses hid my hiding-place;
Grasses run like a green sea
O'er the lawn up to my knee.

Under grass alone he lies,
10 Looking up with leaden eyes,
Scarlet coat and pointed gun,
To the stars and to the sun.

When the grass is ripe like grain,
When the scythe[1] is stoned again,
15 When the lawn is shaven clear,
Then my hole shall reappear.

I shall find him, never fear,
I shall find my grenadier[2];
But, for all that's gone and come,
20 I shall find my soldier dumb[3].

He has lived, a little thing,
In the grassy woods of spring;
Done, if he could tell me true,
Just as I should like to do.

25 He has seen the starry hours
And the springing of the flowers;
And the fairy things that pass
In the forests of the grass.

---

[1]**scythe:** a tool used to cut grass or crops, such as wheat

[2]**grenadier:** a soldier

[3]**dumb:** someone or something that cannot talk

UNIT 2 ▨▨▨▨▨▨▨▨▨▨▨▨▨▨▨▨▨▨▨▨▨▨▨▨▨▨▨▨
Key Ideas and Details

84

In the silence he has heard
30 Talking bee and ladybird[4],
And the butterfly has flown
O'er him as he lay alone.

Not a word will he disclose,
Not a word of all he knows.
35 I must lay him on the shelf,
And make up the tale myself.

1 The speaker, or main character, in this poem is *most* likely ____.

    A a father

    B an old man

    C a young boy

    D an toy soldier

2 Interpret what the speaker, or main character, is concerned about doing.

    A He is concerned about when to bury his toys.

    B He is concerned about why he cares about toys.

    C He is concerned about where to bury his toy soldier.

    D He is concerned about what his toy soldier has seen.

3 Analyze how the speaker feels about his toy soldier.

_____

_____

_____

_____

_____

[4]**ladybird:** a red beetle with black spots, also called a ladybug

UNIT 2
Key Ideas and Details

85

4 Explain why the speaker puts his toy soldier in a hole.

_____

_____

_____

_____

_____

5 Interpret the last stanza. What kind of tale do you think the speaker will tell for the soldier?

_____

_____

_____

_____

_____

UNIT 2 ▪▪▪
Key Ideas and Details

Analyzing Events and Concepts

RI.4.3, RI.4.7

Vocabulary

asthma

Inca

tsunami

volcano

Nothing happens on its own. People, events, and ideas all relate to and interact with one another. When you read, you have to think about the relationships between events, ideas, and people. This helps you better understand the stories, facts, and other texts that you read.

As you read, think about the order in which events happen. Also, think about why certain events happen. To find the cause of an event, you can ask yourself, "Why did that happen?" To find the effect, you can ask, "What happened?"

Guided Practice

Read the passage. Then answer the questions.

Inca
South American Indian people living in the central Andes before the Spanish conquest

Where Did We Get Potatoes?

by Stacy Rummel

You may eat potatoes with most of your meals. Did you ever think about how we got potatoes?

In 500 BC, the ancient Inca people lived in South America. They worshipped their potatoes. They called them "fruit of the earth." Potatoes helped them survive in times of war or famine. In fact, the Inca people sometimes buried their dead with potatoes.

How did Americans find them? The story is that Spanish explorers went looking for gold in Peru in 1532. They saw the Inca eating *chuñu*. The Inca had found ways to store potatoes. They would dry them and mash them. Potatoes could be stored for up to ten years! This was *chuñu*. The explorers learned about potatoes and kept them on their boats.

By 1570, Spanish farmers grew potatoes to feed their animals. In the late 1500s, potatoes could be seen across Europe. Many people were scared to eat them at first. Even poor people were nervous about eating them. They thought that witches made them. Many only fed them to their animals.

Potatoes were not really eaten until the late 1700s. King Louis XVI planted them in his field. He wanted the people of France to grow them. He had guards watching over his potatoes. People said that anything that was guarded must be good. People took potato plants from him at night. They planted them on their farms. This was what the king had wanted!

Potatoes were introduced to the United States many times and in many places during the 1600s. In 1719, settlers planted them in New Hampshire. From there, they spread across the country.

Our country is proud of its Idaho potatoes. This was actually a type of potato that the Europeans brought with them. In fact, settlers taught the Native Americans to grow them in 1836.

Now potatoes are a popular food. We use them in many dishes. We enjoy them in soup, mashed, roasted, fried, baked, and the list goes on.

Who discovered the Inca eating *chuñu?*

A   King Louis XVI

B   Spanish explorers

C   settlers

D   Spanish farmers

This is a detail you can find directly in the text. "Spanish explorers went looking for gold in Peru in 1532. They saw the Inca eating *chuñu.*" Choice B is the correct answer. King Louis XVI, settlers, and Spanish farmers did not find the Inca eating *chuñu.*

According to the passage, which of these events happened *first?*

A   The Incas showed the Spanish explorers *chuñu.*

B   King Louis XVI planted potatoes in his field.

C   Settlers taught Native Americans how to plant potatoes.

D   The Incas worshipped potatoes and buried them with the dead.

Knowing the **sequence** of events is important. They help you understand what happened. The passage is written in the order in which events happened. You can use the dates to help you understand the order of events. A date like 1570 comes before the 1700s. Choice D is the correct answer.

UNIT 2 ✖✖✖✖✖✖✖✖✖✖✖✖✖✖✖✖✖✖✖✖✖✖✖✖✖✖✖✖✖✖✖✖✖✖✖✖
Key Ideas and Details

Explain how you can tell that many people before the late 1700s did not think that potatoes were good to eat.

_____

_____

_____

✓ This question may take some thought. It's a question in which you need to **draw a conclusion** from details in the article and from what you already know. Here is a sample answer:

Many people before the late 1700s were scared to eat potatoes. Even poor people would not eat them because they thought they came from witches. Potatoes were mostly fed to animals before then.

Analyze the effects of King Louis's plan to encourage people to grow and eat potatoes.

_____

_____

_____

_____

✓ You need to ask yourself, "Was his plan helpful or harmful?" Here is a sample answer:

Yes, the effects were good. He planted them in his field, and then had guards make sure no one stole them. The people thought that anything worth guarding must be good. They wanted them. They stole them at night and planted them on their farms. This is what the king wanted to happen. His plan was successful.

Deluxe Mashed Potatoes

4 large russet potatoes

1 (3 ounce) package cream cheese, softened

$\frac{1}{2}$ cup sour cream

1 tablespoon chopped chives

$\frac{3}{4}$ teaspoon onion salt

$\frac{1}{4}$ teaspoon pepper

1 tablespoon butter or margarine

paprika

1. Peel and cube the potatoes. Place the potatoes in a saucepan and cover them with water. Cook the potatoes over medium heat until tender and drain.

2. Mash the potatoes until smooth (do not add milk or butter).

3. Stir in cream cheese, sour cream, chives, onion salt, and pepper.

4. Spoon the potatoes into a greased $1\frac{1}{2}$ quart baking dish. Dot the potatoes with butter and sprinkle with paprika, if desired.

5. Cover and bake at 350°F for 35–40 minutes, or until heated through.

Which of these steps do you do *first?*

A   Mash the potatoes until smooth.

B   Cover and bake at 350°F.

C   Peel and cube the potatoes.

D   Stir in chives.

Cooking involves following step-by-step directions. Each step has a relationship to the next. If you miss a step or do them out of order, you could end up with food that doesn't taste great. If you read the recipe carefully, you'll see that choices A, B, and D are all steps that come *after* peeling and cubing the potatoes. Choice C is the correct answer.

Determine which of these should *not* be done before step 5.

   A   Measure the cream cheese, sour cream, chives, onion salt, and pepper.

   B   Grease a baking dish.

   C   Serve the potatoes.

   D   Preheat the oven.

This question asks you to make an inference. Cooks have to follow steps, but sometimes a recipe does not list every step. Cooks make inferences about what tasks they need to do before they can complete another step. Choices A, B, and D are all steps that should be done before step 5. The correct answer is choice C.

Explain what could happen if you didn't do step 2.

_____

_____

_____

This question asks you to **make a prediction.** You know that making mashed potatoes involves actually mashing the potatoes. If you didn't mash the potatoes, you would have cubed potatoes. Here is a sample answer:

   The potatoes you made would not be mashed potatoes. They would be cubed potatoes, or very lumpy, with the other ingredients in them.

Considering *both* this recipe and the article, why do you think people began to make mashed potatoes?

_____

_____

_____

_____

This question asks you to think about the recipe and what you learned in the article. Do you remember that the Inca dried their potatoes to store them longer? They then mashed them to make *chuñu*. The Incas had been eating a form of mashed potatoes long ago. Here is a sample answer:

People wanted a different way to be able to eat potatoes. They may have gotten tired of eating them the same way they had been cooking them, so they tried new recipes. Mashed potatoes are one way to use potatoes that people enjoy.

Read the passage. Then answer the questions.

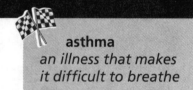

asthma
an illness that makes it difficult to breathe

An Unlikely Winner

Amy Van Dyken was born in Colorado. She was born on February 15, 1973. When Amy was a young girl, her doctor told her that she had asthma. This meant that sometimes she could not catch her breath. Being in gym class or running outside in the cold sometimes made her short of breath. People who have asthma need to stay on medication. When Amy was 6 years old, her doctor wanted her to try swimming, too. He said the warm water would help Amy's breathing. It would help her in daily tasks and allow her to play sports.

Amy did not get better right away. She trained hard. She was finally able to swim the length of an Olympic-sized pool when she was 13. Her high school team thought she was a slow swimmer. Other swimmers didn't want to swim with her. Amy tried even harder.

She spent her first two years of college at the University of Arizona. She won a silver medal at the National Collegiate Athletic Association (NCAA) Championships in 1993. Amy knew she could do even better. She left Arizona for Colorado State University. At the 1994 NCAA Championships, she won a gold medal. Amy was also named NCAA

UNIT 2
Key Ideas and Details

Swimmer of the Year. Amy decided to take time off from college to train for the 1996 Olympics.

At the 1996 Summer Olympics in Atlanta, Georgia, Amy won four gold medals. Two were for individual events. Two were for relays. She was the first female swimmer to win four gold medals in one Olympics. What is so amazing about this? Amy's lungs could only take in 65% of a normal person's capacity because of her asthma. Fans loved Amy because of her likable personality and honesty. After she won gold in the 50-meter freestyle, Amy said, "This is a victory for all the nerds." She said this because many people with asthma cannot be in sports.

Amy graduated from college in 1997. Then she competed at the world championships. Here she won three gold medals. In 1998, while lifting weights, she hurt her shoulder. Surgery followed. Many people thought Amy would never swim again. Amy didn't have another plan. She had overcome problems with asthma. She wasn't going to let an injury keep her from swimming again. Amy started training for the 2000 Summer Olympics in Sydney, Australia. She won two gold medals.

Amy was the only American swimmer to enter into the Swimming Hall of Fame in 2007. In 2008, she also became part of the Olympic Hall of Fame.

Identify which of these events happened *first.*

A Amy won four gold medals at the 1996 Olympics.

B Amy's doctor wanted her to start swimming when she was 6.

C Amy won two gold medals at the 2000 Olympics.

D Amy was entered into the Swimming Hall of Fame in 2007.

This passage organizes events in the order that they happened, or chronological order. By looking at the dates of the events, you know that the correct answer is choice B. The other events happened after Amy was 6 years old.

Explain why Amy's doctor wanted her to start swimming.

_____

_____

_____

 This question asks you to find a reason something happened. It asks you to identify **cause and effect.** The effect was that Amy started swimming. A detail in the passage identifies the cause. Here is a sample answer:

> *Amy could not do the same things that other kids could do. She had asthma. Swimming would help Amy to do daily tasks and allow her to play sports. Swimming would help her breathing.*

Why did Amy leave college after only three years?

  A   She wanted to train for the Olympics.

  B   She wanted to become a swim coach.

  C   She hurt her shoulder.

  D   She had surgery.

 Here again, you're asked to identify a cause. The effect was that Amy left college. You can look back in the text to read why she left if you can't remember. She didn't leave to become a swim coach. Her shoulder was hurt and she had surgery later in her career. Choice A is the correct answer.

According to the article, how did Amy's asthma help her overcome her shoulder injury?

_____

_____

_____

_____

 Here you need to think about the whole article. How did asthma help Amy? What did people think after Amy's surgery? Here is a sample answer:

Many thought Amy wouldn't swim again. Amy had overcome asthma to become a good swimmer. She wouldn't let an injury keep her from swimming again. Because Amy had to overcome asthma to swim, she knew she could overcome anything, even a shoulder injury.

Tsunami!

Have you heard the word *tsunami?* A tsunami is many large waves that come after an earthquake. It could also come after a volcano erupts under the sea. The waves move in all directions after the disruption.

What happens when you throw a rock into a pond? You make ripples in the water. However, the waves from a tsunami can move up to 500 miles an hour! When they reach the shore, the waves can be as high as 100 feet. That is as tall as a 10-story building!

Which state is most likely to have a tsunami? Hawaii. Hawaii has about one tsunami a year. About every seven years, a tsunami causes damage in Hawaii. In 1946, a tsunami in Hawaii flooded the downtown streets of Hilo, Hawaii.

What should you do if you live near the Pacific Coast and there is an earthquake? Turn on a radio that runs on batteries. Listen for a tsunami warning or other instructions. Sometimes the weather service will warn people to leave the area.

The best way to protect yourself is to listen for an early warning that a tsunami is coming. There are tsunami warning centers in Hawaii that tell people when a tsunami is coming. People can then leave their homes and get away from the ocean.

If you have pets, you need to think about what you will do with them in a tsunami. It is best to take all pets with you if you have to leave your home. If you stay at an emergency shelter, pets may not be able to stay with you. Check if there are hotels near you that are "pet friendly" and allow pets. Being prepared is your best plan!

tsunami
many waves that come after an earthquake or other disturbance under the sea

volcano
mountain or hill with a crater or vent through which lava, rock, and gas may erupt from Earth's crust

1 Determine which of these is the *first* thing you should do if you live near the Pacific Coast and there is an earthquake.

   A Find a place for your pets to stay.

   B Turn on the radio.

   C Go to the beach.

   D Turn off the lights.

2 For a tsunami to form, there must *first* be ____.

   A lightning

   B a thunderstorm

   C a hurricane and flood

   D an undersea earthquake

3 The *best* protection from a tsunami is to ____.

   A stay inside instead of leaving the area

   B sit on the shore watching for waves

   C listen for an early warning that a tsunami is coming

   D live in a building that is less than 100 feet

4 Explain what causes a tsunami.

_____

_____

_____

_____

5 Explain why states like Illinois and Nebraska do not need to be concerned about a tsunami.

_____

_____

_____

_____

REVIEW

Key Ideas and Details

Vocabulary
aroma
detour
immigrant

aroma
the smell of food being cooked

detour
a forced change in direction

Read the passage. Then answer the questions.

Why Anansi the Spider Has Eight Thin Legs

a retelling of an African fable

Long ago, there lived a spider named Anansi. His wife was a great cook, but Anansi liked to sample the food that his friends in the village prepared and cooked.

As he strolled to the village, Anansi took a detour to his friend Rabbit's house. He could smell an enchanting scent coming from Rabbit's stove.

"What is that fragrant smell?" Anansi asked Rabbit.

"They are greens," Rabbit replied. "They aren't completely done yet, so why don't you stay and eat with me?"

Anansi knew if he stayed at Rabbit's house, Rabbit would give him jobs to do. Anansi didn't want to do any work for Rabbit, but he had a brilliant idea.

"I'll spin a web and tie one end of it around my leg and one end to your pot. When the greens are done cooking, pull on the web, and I'll know to come back." Rabbit promised Anansi he would do just that.

"I smell beans!" Anansi thought as he rambled on his journey. Just then, he noticed his friends the monkeys. Father Monkey's children were flying from tree to tree above Anansi.

"Anansi! It is good to see you," said Father Monkey. "Won't you stay and join us for some delicious beans? They are almost done cooking, and I know they are one of your favorites."

"Beans would be wonderful!" said Anansi. He explained to Father Monkey that he would attach one end of his web to his leg and the other end to the pot of beans.

"Oh, that is a most wonderful idea, Anansi!" said Father Monkey. "You are a clever spider!"

As Anansi continued to roam, he smelled the aroma of delicious sweet potatoes.

"Sweet potatoes and honey—what a treat!" Anansi said aloud.

"I hear your voice, Anansi," said his friend Hog. "Please stop and eat some with me. I would appreciate your company today."

Anansi told Hog of his brilliant idea.

"I love that idea," cried Hog. Hog tied one end of Anansi's web to his pot of sweet potatoes and promised Anansi he would let him know when they were finished cooking.

When Anansi finally made it to the river, he had smelled so many delicious foods that he had one web tied to each of his eight legs. Anansi felt a yank at his leg. It was the web tied to Rabbit's greens. Just then, he felt another tug. Then he felt another pull. Anansi was being pulled in many directions at once!

"What am I to do?" thought Anansi.

When he felt the fourth and fifth strings pull, he knew he had a major problem. Suddenly, the rest of the strings were being pulled. Everyone was pulling him at the same time. What should Anansi do?

Anansi did the best he could to roll into the river. Slowly, the webs washed away, and Anansi crawled back on the sandy shore.

"What have I done to myself?" Anansi said as he looked at himself. "I don't think my idea was such a brilliant one," Anansi cried.

To this day, Anansi the Spider has eight thin legs.

1 Determine which of these is the *best* moral of this story.

   A Friends are blind.

   B It all depends on your point of view.

   C You shouldn't expect to get something for nothing.

   D Don't ask anyone else to solve your problems for you.

2 Anansi tries to be _____.

   A who he is not

   B mean to everyone

   C hungry all the time

   D everywhere at once

3 Read the paragraph below.

> *When he felt the fourth and fifth strings pull, he knew he had a major problem. Suddenly, the rest of the strings were being pulled. Everyone was pulling him at the same time. What should Anansi do?*

Determine the topic sentence of the paragraph.

   A All of a sudden the rest of the strings were being pulled.

   B When he felt the fourth and fifth strings pull, he knew he had a major problem.

   C Everyone was pulling him at the same time.

   D What should Anansi do?

4 Why did Anansi tie one end of his web to Rabbit's pot?

   A He wanted to know when the food was done but did not want to wait.

   B Rabbit wasn't going to be home.

   C He wanted to be able to get back to Rabbit's house.

   D Rabbit needed help cooking.

5 Anansi's friends lived in _____.

   A the jungle

   B the forest

   C a village

   D a large city

UNIT 2 ✖✖✖✖✖✖✖✖✖✖
Key Ideas and Details

6 Analyze the reason this story might have been written.

    A to give a reader new recipes

    B to help students try new foods

    C to explain an important lesson

    D to tell about the foods spiders like to eat

7 Which of these details does *not* belong in a summary of the story?

    A Father Monkey's children were flying from tree to tree above Anansi.

    B Anasi liked to taste the food that his friends cooked.

    C Anansi didn't want to do any work for Rabbit, so he told him of a plan that would allow Rabbit to tell him when the greens were done.

    D When Anansi finally made it to the river, he had one web tied to each of his eight legs.

8 We know that Anansi is greedy because of what _____.

    A he says

    B he does

    C the narrator tells us

    D the other characters tell us

9 Analyze the story. At the end of the story, does Anansi get what he deserves?

_____

_____

_____

_____

_____

Jane Addams's Hull House

Jane Addams's childhood prepared her for the work she would do helping others when she was a young woman. Jane grew up in a nice house. She had clean clothes to wear and room to run and play near her home.

When she was 2 years old, Jane's mom died. As a young girl, Jane got sick and it caused her to have a misshaped spine. Childhood events left Jane with love for people who suffered as she had.

On a trip to visit one of her father's businesses near Chicago, Jane saw how people were living. They had very small homes. Children were wearing dirty clothes. They played in the streets. Jane learned that these people didn't have any money to move into better homes. Jane made a decision. She decided that when she was older, she was going to help poor people.

Jane graduated from Rockford Seminary in 1881. After college, women had two choices. They could marry and have children or become a teacher. Jane didn't want to do either. It took her nearly eight years to find her calling.

In 1888, Jane visited Toynbee Hall in London. It was set up to help poor people. When she left, Jane knew what she wanted to do.

Jane and her friend, Ellen Gates Starr, rented a large house in Chicago. It once belonged to Charles Hull. Immigrants lived near her home. These were people who came from Europe and hoped for a better life in America. These were the same poor families she had seen when she was a little girl.

immigrant
a person who leaves his own country to live in another country

The immigrants often lived in terrible conditions. Their crowded apartments were dirty. Many did not speak English. They worked in factories that paid very little money.

One of Hull House's first projects was to provide childcare services for families that had to work but had nowhere to leave their children. Until then, many parents left young children in their apartment by themselves. Older children worked, too, or walked the streets while their parents were working. Childcare kept the children safe while their parents were gone during the day.

After that, Hull House also began to hold classes for immigrants. These classes taught immigrants how to speak English, cook, sew, and other important skills they needed. People came to Hull House to meet with neighbors and socialize.

In 1931, Jane won a Nobel Peace Prize for her work. By the time she died in 1935, Hull House took up the entire block. Many middle-class women had come to help Jane and Ellen at Hull House. Today, many community centers like Hull House help the poor in their own neighborhoods.

10 According to the author, how did Jane's childhood prepare her for her work at Hull House?

_____

_____

_____

_____

11 What specific event led Jane to open Hull House?

A Jane saw immigrants that needed help.

B Jane visited Toynbee Hall in London.

C Ellen said she would help her.

D Jane graduated from college.

12 Determine which of these is the topic sentence of paragraph 3.

A On a trip to visit one of her father's businesses near Chicago, Jane saw how people were living.

B Children were wearing dirty clothes.

C Jane learned that these people didn't have any money to move into better homes.

D She decided that when she was older, she was going to help poor people.

13 Hull House is located in _____.

A Europe

B London

C Rockford

D Chicago

14 What was the *main* reason Hull House provided childcare to working families?

    A People had nowhere to leave their children while they worked.

    B Childcare was too expensive for immigrants.

    C There weren't enough babysitters.

    D There were no schools.

15 Hull House began classes for immigrants ____.

    A after they started offering childcare

    B before they started offering childcare

    C before Jane finished college

    D after Jane won the Nobel Peace Prize

16 Based on the article, which of these was *not* one of the goals of Hull House?

    A to teach immigrants English and other skills

    B to help rich people

    C to help poor people

    D to take care of children

17 Write a summary of the passage. Include only the main ideas and most important details.

_____

_____

_____

_____

_____

Craft and Structure

Writing is more than putting words on paper. It is a craft. It is a little like building something. A writer carefully chooses words. He thinks about why he is writing. He thinks about the reader. Then he puts together words into sentences. Then he builds sentences into paragraphs. Finally, paragraphs join together to create something bigger.

● **In Lesson 8,** you'll learn how writers build stories, poems, songs, and plays. You'll learn how stories are made of sentences, paragraphs, and chapters. Then you will see how poems are made of lines and stanzas and how scenes fit together to build plays. You will see how writers tell a story, or show how a character grows and learns.

● **Lesson 9** is about craft and structure in information texts. You'll learn about the ways that writers give facts and details to their readers. How writers build their writing depends on what they want you to know.

● **Lesson 10** is about point of view. You'll understand how writers use their own point of view. Writers also give characters their own points of view. *How* a story or facts are told depends on the author's purpose or what the author wants to tell. The point of view can shape the way you read. It can shape the way you understand and feel towards texts. In this lesson, you will learn how to recognize the author's point of view in informational text.

Literary Structure

RL.4.5

Vocabulary

docked

foreman

premature

tarriers

tay

tenement

When you read, do you notice how the text is organized? All text has a structure. A book has chapters. A play has acts and scenes, and a poem has stanzas. These elements build on one another to create the larger work. These literary works are structured to make you want to read on to find out what happens in the text. The author also uses images and ideas to support a theme. Sentences or lines of dialogue work together to reveal something about a character. Stanzas in a poem may parallel each other or they may offer a contrast. Recognizing the structure of a text helps increase your enjoyment and understanding of it.

Guided Practice

Read the song lyrics. Then answer the questions.

Drill, Ye Tarriers, Drill

an American folk song of the 1880s

Every morning about seven o'clock
There's twenty tarriers[1] a workin' at the rock
The boss comes along and he says, "Keep still
And come down heavy on the cast iron drill."

Chorus
And drill, ye tarriers, drill
Drill, ye tarriers, drill
For it's work all day for the sugar in your tay[2]
Down beyond the railway
And drill, ye tarriers, drill
And blast, and fire.

---

[1]**tarriers:** Irish workers whose job was to drill holes in rock to blast out railroad tunnels

[2]**tay:** tea

The foreman[3]'s name was John McCann
By gosh, he was a blamed mean man
Last week a premature[4] blast went off
And a mile in the air went big Jim Goff.

Repeat chorus

And when next payday came around
Jim Goff a dollar short was found
When he asked, "What for?" came this reply
"You were docked[5] for the time you were up in the sky."

Repeat chorus

Tarriers live on work and sweat
There ain't no tarrier got rich yet
Sleep and work, then work some more
And we'll drill right through to the core.

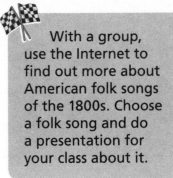

With a group, use the Internet to find out more about American folk songs of the 1800s. Choose a folk song and do a presentation for your class about it.

Folk songs are stories about a community of people and what is important to them. Folk songs were spread by word of mouth. They were the music of the working class. Poems are made of lines and stanzas. The lines of this folk song contain both rhythm and rhyme. People sing choruses between the verses, or stanzas, of a song. In this folk song, the chorus follows each stanza.

Like poems, folk songs also have rhyme and rhythm. You can clap the rhythm of a song or poem. You usually start with an unstressed and then a stressed beat, so you clap on syllables. In the line, "And when payday came around," you would clap on the syllables *when, pay, came,* and *round.* These are four beats of rhythm.

[3]**foreman:** boss

[4]**premature:** too early

[5]**docked:** money taken from pay for being late or bad behavior

Interpret the main idea of each stanza.

Stanza 1 _____

_____

Stanza 2 _____

_____

Stanza 3 _____

_____

Stanza 4 _____

_____

✔ Did you notice how each stanza of this folk song is like a chapter in a book? Each stanza has a main idea. The first stanza explains the setting and introduces the *main characters*. Workers are drilling into rock. They need to drill through mountains to build the railroad. The second stanza describes the workers' boss. The third stanza gives an example of how unfair the foreman is. In the fourth stanza, the tarriers keep working in spite of the hardships. They will not give up.

Your answers should tell about the structure of the folk song and what happens in each stanza. Here is a sample answer:

Stanza 1—The tarriers begin their work early in the day. They are drilling to build the railroad. The foreman, or boss, tells them they need to work harder.

Stanza 2—The workers describe their boss as a mean man. They also say that a worker named Jim Goff was blown into the sky when a dynamite blast went off too soon.

Stanza 3— On payday, Jim Goff discovers that he has less pay. The boss tells him he received less pay because he was not working when he was in the air. The workers think the boss is unfair. They also lose pay for any reason.

Stanza 4—The workers just get back to the job. They know their job is unfair, but they can't change that. They have little choice but to keep working.

UNIT 3 ▓▓▓▓▓▓▓▓▓▓▓▓▓▓▓▓▓▓▓▓▓▓▓▓▓▓▓▓▓▓▓▓▓▓▓▓
Craft and Structure

The structure of a folk song is *most* like a ____.

A play

C mystery

B fairy tale

D poem

A folk song is not like a play, fairy tale, or mystery. It is like a poem. Most poems have lines and stanzas, or verses. Songs usually also have a chorus. The correct answer is choice D.

Analyze the folk song. How does the chorus contribute to the overall theme of the folk song?

_____

_____

_____

_____

The chorus repeats just as the men repeat the same hard work day after day. A work song helps them share their feelings. It helps them keep working hard. Here is a sample answer:

The chorus tells how hard the tarriers' job is. It is not easy to drill through rock day after day. The words "drill, drill" help the reader understand this. However, the tarriers know they have little choice. They must keep drilling if they want to earn money.

Choose any stanza of the folk song. Which lines in the stanza rhyme?

A Lines 1 and 3 rhyme, and lines 2 and 4 rhyme.

B Lines 1 and 2 rhyme, and lines 3 and 4 rhyme.

C Lines 1 and 4 rhyme, and lines 2 and 3 rhyme.

D Lines 2 and 3 rhyme, and lines 1 and 4 rhyme.

In each stanza, or verse, the first and second lines rhyme, and the third and fourth lines rhyme. The correct answer is choice B.

Read the following line.

For it's work all day for the sugar in your tay

Interpret the meaning of this line.

_____

_____

_____

 In this folk song, "sugar in your tay" has a deeper meaning. Poets often use metaphors to convey a deeper meaning. Here is a sample answer:

> This line means that the tarriers are working very hard for very little money. They do not have money for things that are fun or special. They can barely afford little luxuries, like sugar for their tea.

Read the play. Then answer the questions.

"Time's a-Wasting!"

tenement
a building in the poorer part of a city that has apartments or rooms for rent

CHARACTERS:

Mother Finn and her children, recent Irish immigrants

Mike Finn, Mother Finn's oldest son

Murphy, a recruiter for the Union Pacific Railroad

Darby, Gallagher, Dunn, and Maguire, Irish immigrant railroad workers

Sullivan, railroad job site boss

Scene 1

With the help of her children, Mother Finn, an Irish immigrant, is hanging wash on a clothesline behind the family's rundown New York City tenement building. Mike, her oldest, is carrying a heavy basket of wet clothes. The year is 1864.

MOTHER FINN: Time's a wasting, children, let us get all this washing hung up to dry. There is ironing yet to do and packages of laundry to bundle.

MURPHY *(approaching the family with a handbill in his hand, tipping his hat to Mother Finn):* Top of the morning to you, Mrs. Finn! It is a beautiful day in America! A strong young man you have there,

Mother Finn. You must feed him well. A strapping young lad makes a strong and able worker I always say.

MURPHY *(addressing Mike Finn):* What is your name, lad?

MIKE FINN *(setting down the basket of laundry):* Name is Mike, Mike Finn.

MURPHY *(shaking hands):* Murphy is my name. It is a pleasure to meet you, lad. Would a fine young lad like you be looking for a job? *(waving the rolled-up handbill in the air)* Look at what it says right here, Mike Finn. I think I just might be able to help you.

MOTHER FINN: I do what I can, but taking in washing barely puts enough food on the table.

MIKE FINN: Aye, my poor mother is doing all she can since my father passed away.

MURPHY: Well, lucky you are that I came along. *(unrolling the handbill)* Look here, lad, the Union Pacific Railroad is looking for strong young men. You could play a part in building a railroad across America! The Union Pacific Railroad will pay $8 a month plus food and a place to rest your head. You will be able to send your wages back home to help your poor mother.

MOTHER FINN: My son does not shy away from hard work, Mr. Murphy. But railroad work is too dangerous! Many have died trying to tame the wilderness. I have heard tales of terrible accidents, Indian attacks, outlaws… I cannot let him go!

MIKE FINN *(interrupting his mother):* Ma, I need a job; we need the money, and the railroad is hiring!

MURPHY *(slapping Mike on the back to congratulate him on his decision):* Then it is settled. Your boy has a job, Mrs. Finn! Come with me, lad.

Mike and Murphy leave for the railroad office.

Scene 2

At the railroad work site on the western plains, Darby, Gallagher, and Maguire are taking a break from their work.

DARBY *(removing his cap and wiping his brow with his sleeve):* Blazing sun is about to do me in! Days on the western plains are long and hot.

GALLAGHER: To be sure they are, mate. Today is as blazing as the winter is frigid. We lost three men in that last blizzard. Poor souls froze to death!

DARBY *(shivering):* That is enough to make a roasted man shiver!

MAGUIRE *(taking a ladleful of water out of a bucket to have a drink):* I would rather suffer with the heat and cold than have another brush with Indians. Poor old Dunn did not know what hit him when that band of Sioux warriors raided our camp.

Use the library or the Internet to find more information about the immigrants, freed slaves, and former Union and Confederate soldiers who built the Transcontinental Railroad.

DARBY: I hope we survive working for the Union Pacific Railroad Company.

MAGUIRE: Aye, toil as we may, there is little glory for the man who works on the railroad.

DARBY: We had best be getting back to work, lads. Sullivan is looking in our direction.

The three men cast aside their dinner pails, pick up their tools, and get back to work.

MAGUIRE: He must have found a new recruit—another strong young lad from out East. Poor innocent lad doesn't know what he's in for.

GALLAGHER: No doubt, the Union Pacific has promised much. Little does he know that he will be working for months to pay the railroad back for the train fare.

DARBY: Put some muscle to your shovels, mates. Foreman Sullivan and the boy are heading this way.

SULLIVAN *(looking over the work site and assessing their progress):* You lads have a long way to go until quitting time. *(nodding toward Finn)* This here is Mike Finn. He is new to railroading—just off the train from way back East this morning. Says he's ready to work.

MIKE FINN *(shaking hands with each of the men):* Pleasure to meet all of you.

SULLIVAN: I am putting Finn on your crew. Darby, I am asking you to watch out for this lad. Show him how to use that sledge, and keep him working. We do not want anything to happen to the lad. We need to keep him working long enough to repay his one-way fare!

SULLIVAN *(addressing all four men):* Get back to work, lads! It's ten miles of track a day, come what may. We are building Mr. Lincoln's railroad clear across America. Get busy, lads, time's a-wasting!

Which of the following is the *most* important thing the author wants you to know from the beginning of the play?

    A   Mother Finn has a laundry business.

    B   The railroads recruited poor immigrant workers.

    C   Mike Finn is healthy and strong.

    D   This play takes place during the Civil War.

> The railroads looked for poor immigrant workers because they would work for less money. Recruiters, like Murphy, could fool them easily. They would tell the immigrants that the work was an adventure. The other answers are true. However, you can tell from scene 1 that the play is about the railroad recruiters. The correct answer is choice B.

Analyze scene 1 of the play. What is the conflict in this scene?

_____

_____

_____

_____

_____

> The conflict is the problem in the story or play. Here is a sample answer:

We know that the Finn family is poor. They are working hard to earn money. The recruiter, Murphy, creates the conflict. He promises Mike money and adventure. Mike wants to work on the railroad because he wants to help his family. However, Mother Finn does not want her son to work on the railroad because it is dangerous.

Explain how the conflict builds in scene 2. What do you predict might happen in the next scene?

_____

_____

_____

_____

_____

✓ **Here is a sample answer:**

      In scene 2, the railroad workers are unhappy. The conflict is between what the workers were promised and what they received. The workers were promised many things, but they were given nothing. If the play continues, we know there will be more conflict. Mike Finn will most likely feel betrayed. We know this is true because the other railroad workers feel betrayed because the railroad did not keep its promise.

Scenes 1 and 2 take place about 2,000 miles apart. Compare the two settings.

_____

_____

_____

_____

✓ **Here is a sample answer:**

      Scene 1 is outside a tenement building in the city. Scene 2 takes place at a railroad work site on the western plains. Both scenes are set in poor and difficult conditions. The workers in both settings are working hard for little pay.

How do you think Mike Finn feels about the two settings?

_____

_____

_____

 Here is a sample answer:

> You wonder if Mike Finn can adjust to the changes in his life. You wonder how he will feel about the hard work and harsh conditions. Scene 1 is familiar to Mike Finn. He is with his loving mother and family. Scene 2 is far from home. Here he must answer to Foreman Sullivan and the railroad company. He most likely is worried about doing well on the job. Mike probably misses his family.

Think about how the phrase "time's a-wasting" is used in the play. How does the meaning change from scene 1 to scene 2?

_____

_____

_____

 Two different characters use the phrase in the play. However, each character means something different when they use the phrase. Here is a sample answer:

> In scene 1, Mother Finn uses it in a loving way to ask her children for their help. Her children can help her by making her work go faster and easier. She cares about making money to raise her family. They are working together for a common goal. In scene 2, Foreman Sullivan uses the same phrase. However, he seems to mean that time is money. He wants his men to work harder and get the job done faster. He does not care about his men. He cares about finishing the job. The railroad wants to make money.

Three Wise Old Women

by Elizabeth T. Corbett

Three wise old women were they, were they,
Who went to walk on a winter day:
One carried a basket to hold some berries,
One carried a ladder to climb for cherries,
5 The third, and she was the wisest one,
Carried a fan to keep off the sun.

But they went so far, and they went so fast,
They quite forgot their way at last,
So one of the wise women cried in a fright,
10 "Suppose we should meet a bear tonight!
Suppose he should eat me!" "And me!!" "And me!!!"
"What is to be done?" cried all the three.

"Dear, dear!" said one, "we'll climb a tree,
There out of the way of the bears we'll be,"
15 But there wasn't a tree for miles around;
They were too frightened to stay on the ground,
So they climbed their ladder up to the top,
And sat there screaming "We'll drop! We'll drop!"

But the wind was strong as wind could be,
20 And blew their ladder right out to sea;
So the three wise women were all afloat
In a leaky ladder instead of a boat,
And every time the waves rolled in,
Of course the poor things were wet to the skin.

25 Then they took their basket, the water to bale,
They put up their fan instead of a sail:
But what became of the wise women then,
Whether they ever sailed home again,
Whether they saw any bears, or no,
30 You must find out, for I don't know.

"Three Wise Women" is a narrative poem, a poem that tells a story. Summarize each stanza. Then explain how each stanza relates to the others to tell the story. Use terms that you learned in Lesson 6, such as *conflict* and *rising action*.

1 Stanza 1

_____

_____

_____

2 Stanza 2

_____

_____

_____

3 Stanza 3

_____

_____

_____

4 Stanza 4

_____

_____

_____

5 Stanza 5

_____

_____

_____

Text Features

RI.4.5

Vocabulary

intersections

laser

overland

rival

toll

turnstile

Just as stories, poems, and plays have a structure, so, too, does informational text. An author structures his text to best present and support his ideas and information. There are many ways that an author can organize text. There are also various text features that an author can use to make the text easier to read and understand.

Sequence and Chronological Order

Some informational text is presented in **sequence.** Recipes and how-to text use this type of structure. The information is presented in steps or in the order in which tasks must be completed.

| Turn on the DVD player. | → | Open the tray. | → | Place a disc into the tray and close it. | → | Press play on the remote control. |

Information can also be presented in **chronological order.** Biographies and historical accounts may be presented in chronological order. Watch for words that relate to time. These could be dates like *1776* or *2001*, time periods like the *Fifties*, or a specific time like *11:00 p.m.* Sometimes a biography may begin in the present and then flash back to an event that happened earlier in someone's life. Usually, there will be a clue that helps recognize a flashback.

Cause and Effect

Writers often like to show connections between ideas and events. This helps the reader understand the bigger question, *"Why did an event happen?"* It also could answer the question, *"What are the effects of an event?"* Look for *clue words* that signal **cause and effect.** The thing that happens is the **effect.** Why it happens or what made it happen is the **cause.** Look for clue words that signal a cause or an event. Words like *because, since, reason for, due to, on account of* signal why something happened, or what caused it. Clue words like *then, so, led to, as a result, in order that,* and *therefore* signal the effect.

Comparison and Contrast

A third way writers organize writing is to **compare and contrast.** You **compare** when you tell how two things are the same. You **contrast** when you tell how they are different.

This Venn diagram compares and contrasts two electronic devices.

Record player   **Both**   **DVD player**

record spins on a turntable

needle reads bumps on a spiral track on a record

plays sound through speakers

plays different size records

plays a round object

works by reading a spiral track

operates by spinning a disc or record

makes sound

shaped like a box

uses electricity

has a laser, lens, motor, and a computer

plays a small disc

works by remote control

plays sound and video

laser reads a spiral track on a CD

motor spins the disc very fast

The middle of the diagram shows how a record player and a DVD player are the same. It **compares** two things. The outer part of each circle shows how a record player and DVD player are different. They **contrast** two things.

These are some other ways that authors might choose to organize information:

- as a series of problems and solutions
- as a series of questions and answers
- in order of importance, from greatest to least

Can you think of what kinds of information might be presented best with each of these organizational structures?

Help! My DVD Player Won't Work!

The disc loaded but nothing is happening!

- Check that the disc is loaded into the player properly.
- Turn off the player with the disc loaded, unplug the player, then plug it in and turn the player back on.

The disc was playing fine but just stopped working half way through!

- This could be DVD rot. Look for a "coffee stain" on the data side of the disc.
- If you find a stain, the disc is ruined and needs to be replaced.

The video images keep breaking up or freezing!

- Remove the disc and check it for scratches.
- Even if it looks clean, use a DVD cleaning kit to clean the disc.
- DVDs can be cleaned the same way that CDs can, but they are more fragile.

There is no sound! The sound quality is terrible!

- Check the audio connections to be sure that they are secure.
- Replace the cable connecting the DVD unit to your receiver.
- Clean the contacts on the player and receiver with electronic contact cleaner.

The remote control won't work!

- Replace the batteries.
- Get very close to the remote control sensor on the DVD player; try again.
- Turn off the lights in the room. Some long-life energy saver light bulbs can interfere with remote control functions.

The images are out of whack—everyone looks tall and skinny!

- Go to your DVD player's setup menu to find options.
- You will find that this option has been set to "16 x 9."
- Set it to "4 x 3 letterbox," and the images will return to normal.

The disc cover says widescreen, but it is playing in fullscreen!

- The disc cover is wrong, but a disc is encoded to play in either widescreen or fullscreen.
- Enter your DVD player's setup menu and set the aspect ratio option to "4 x 3 letterbox" instead of "4 x 3 Pan & Scan."

The movie subtitles just won't go away!

- Go to your disc's menu and turn off the subtitles.
- Some players will let you turn off subtitles. Do this by pressing the subtitle button on the remote and then pressing 0 or clear.

How a DVD Player Works

laser
device that creates a powerful beam of light

A DVD disc looks like it is made of plastic. However, inside the plastic is a layer of aluminum. Discs seem smooth and solid. However, there are tracks in the layers of plastic. They are like grooves on a record, but they are much, much smaller. There are millions of little bumps in the tracks where data is stored. Instead of a using a needle to read the bumps, a laser shines light through the plastic. Then it reflects the light back to a lens.

DVDs are an effect of a long history of recording. In 1877, Thomas Edison invented the phonograph. This device used discs and cylinders. The sound was scratchy and faint. Yet, it made the very first recording of a human voice. Later, it became known as the record player.

The record player had a needle that followed a spiral track on a record. The first records were made of wax discs. The record player read the bumps and grooves across the wax. Soon, round records were replaced with CDs. Lasers read groves in CDs. The DVD followed shortly after. The DVD recorded music and video. A decoder inside the DVD player changes the data into sound and video signals. Then it sends the signals to your television through cables.

The first passage is organized as ____.

A a chronological sequence

B a series of causes and effects

C a series of questions and answers

D a series of problems and solutions

Electronics, appliances, and machines come with an instruction manual. The manual explains how the machine works. It also includes a troubleshooting guide that tells you how to fix problems with your machine. The correct answer is choice D. Choices A, B, and C are incorrect. Time order (choice A) wouldn't make sense for this passage. A cause-and-effect structure (choice B) would tell you why your DVD player isn't working but not how to fix it. A FAQ structure ("frequently asked questions") asks a common question followed by its answer (choice C).

Explain what you should do if the pictures look funny on your screen.

_____

_____

_____

 Read through the list of problems until you find your problem and its solution. Here is a sample answer:

> Go to the DVD player's setup menu. Find the options submenu for letterbox or pan & scan. Set the option to 4 x 3 letterbox and the image will return to normal.

Determine how the second passage is organized.

A as a comparison of two things

B in chronological sequence of events

C as a series of problem and solution in question format

D as a cause and effect of the phonograph and DVD

 The second passage explains how DVDs work. It does not give problems and solutions. It does not compare and contrast two things. Instead, it shows you through cause and effect how the DVD came to be. There is a clue sentence in the second paragraph: "DVDs are an effect of a long history of recording." The correct answer is D.

Determine a possible solution if you are having problems with the sound quality of your DVD.

_____

_____

_____

_____

✔ First, you need to know which passage to check for the answer. You are looking for a solution. So, you will look at the first passage. This is the problem and solution passage. Then find the section on sound quality. Here is a sample answer:

> Check the audio connections to be sure that they are secure. Replace the cable connecting the DVD unit to your receiver. Clean the contacts on the player and receiver with electronic contact cleaner.

Analyze the first passage. Explain another way the information in this passage could be organized.

_____

_____

_____

✔ Information can be organized in different ways. An author selects the organization that will best suit his readers. Here is a sample answer:

> The first passage is a list of problems and solutions. It could be changed to a question and answer. The problems could be formed into questions. Then the solutions become the answers.

Dr. Martin Cooper, Inventor of the Cell Phone

Way back in 1973 did you know that cell phones would become popular?

Dr. Cooper: I knew that people wanted to be able to talk from anywhere. People like the freedom to talk to other people anytime, not just at home or in the car. I knew that cell phones would be popular with people everywhere.

How did you invent the cell phone?

Dr. Cooper: I was the research manager at Motorola. Our engineers applied for a patent for a "radio telephone system." That was the beginning of the cellular phone.

What did the first cell phone look like?

Dr. Cooper: The first cell phone was made in 1973. It was named the Dyna-Tec. It was huge—almost the size of a shoebox. The battery lasted for only 20 minutes. However, that was fine because the phone weighed two and a half pounds. You couldn't hold it up to your ear that long because it was so heavy! It took ten hours to charge the battery.

Who got the first cell phone call?

Dr. Cooper: I made the first cell phone call from a sidewalk in New York City. I called Joe Engel, my rival in research, the general manager at AT&T. I wanted to let him know that we beat his team. We developed the cell phone first.

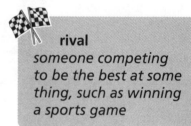

rival
someone competing to be the best at something, such as winning a sports game

Did anyone around you notice what you were doing?

Dr. Cooper: The people standing around me were amazed. In 1973, no one had ever seen someone make a call from a sidewalk using a cell phone. Well, maybe they had seen one in a cartoon or on a funny TV show. Today, just about everyone has a cell phone. It took our company ten years to bring cell phones to market. Finally, cell phones could be sold in stores. Now, more people have cell phones than wired phones.

Which of these *best* describes the structure of this passage?

   A   sequence of steps

   B   questions and answers

   C   cause and effect

   D   compare and contrast

> This passage is a bit different than the ones about DVD players. One of Dr. Cooper's answers tells about a sequence of steps. However, overall it asks questions and Dr. Cooper answers them. It is not cause and effect and not compare and contrast. Choice B is the correct answer.

Read the third question and answer. Explain why Dr. Cooper says that a cell phone battery that lasted for only 20 minutes was fine.

_____

_____

_____

_____

> Dr. Cooper explains the difference between the first cell phone and those we use today. Here is a sample answer:

Dr. Cooper says that "You couldn't hold it up to your ear that long because it was so heavy!" This sentence uses the signal word because. This answer in the interview is organized by cause and effect. Because the phone was so heavy, nobody talked more than 20 minutes.

You have read three different passages. Each had a different organization.
Do you think that there is any one right way to organize a passage?
Support your answer.

_____

_____

_____

_____

_____

_____

 This question asks you for a reasoned opinion. You must also support that opinion. Here is a sample answer.

> You know that organization can help the reader. If you are a writer, you need to think about how to help your reader understand the information. You have to think about what kind of organization would be best for the topic. Sometimes cause and effect may be best for science. Sometimes sequence is best for history. For an interview, a question and answer may be best. But there is no one right way to organize texts.

Test Yourself

Passage 1

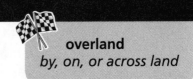

overland
by, on, or across land

America's First Roads

Did you know that the first roads in America were rivers? In colonial America, towns grew along the seacoast and large rivers. Water travel was the way to move people and goods from place to place. People did not travel for fun—very few went far from home. Sometimes overland travel could not be avoided. Rivers did not flow in all the directions people needed to go.

Most paths followed Native American trails. Farmers used these paths to carry goods to market. Narrow dirt paths made travel very difficult and slow. People usually walked. Many roads were so small that carts, even horses, were too big for them. A traveler had to walk and lead the horse down the path!

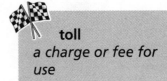

toll
a charge or fee for use

Dirt roads were rough. They were full of ruts and holes, and many people wanted to fix them. Roads near waterways and swamps were fixed first. Rain made these roads extra muddy. Dry weather made other roads dusty. In winter, most roads could not be used.

The first American toll road was paved with wooden planks. It was built in 1786. The wooden planks allowed wheeled carts to roll easily. It kept them from getting stuck in the mud. The traveler paid a fee. Then he went through a turnstile to use the road. Toll roads were built by companies. These companies hoped to get the money they spent building the roads back in tolls.

turnstile
a post with revolving horizontal bars placed at an entrance to allow one person to pass through at a time

In the 1800s, businessmen needed shorter, cheaper ways to send goods across America. In 1818, the first National Road opened to travelers. It was the first federal road. Its nickname was "The Main Street of America." The National Road linked Cumberland, Maryland, to Wheeling, West Virginia (then part of Virginia). Later, it became Route 40.

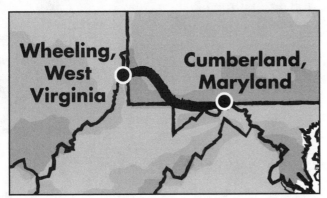

Cities began to pave their busy roads with gravel and cobblestones. They built bridges. However, most roads were still muddy, bumpy dirt tracks. People, horses, bicycles, stray dogs, and other animals shared narrow streets. Roads were crowded.

By 1905, thousands of Americans owned automobiles. Streets were more crowded and more dangerous. New noises frightened horses and pedestrians. Automobiles stalled or broke down. They got stuck in ruts and mud. Roads were too narrow for two cars to move around each other. There were no rules of the road. There were lots of accidents. People and animals were hurt or killed. Drivers were scared. Across the country, people demanded better roads. State governments began to listen. Today, we have roads that connect just about every place you could imagine.

Passage 2

Solving the Problems of America's Roads

The problems with America's roads were not easy to solve. The country needed strong leadership. Solving these problems took time, money, and hard work.

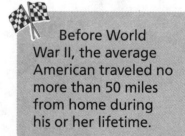

intersections
the places where two roads come together and cross

The first step was taken by the police of New York City. They created "rules of the road." Slow vehicles had to keep to the right. Faster vehicles could pass on the left. Drivers must use hand signals when they turned, stopped, or slowed down.

Another problem was the many accidents that happened at intersections. The first electric traffic signals were installed in the city of Cleveland, Ohio. A red light meant *stop,* and a green light meant *go.* Other cities added traffic signals that had a third color light. This yellow light signaled *caution* or *slow down.*

In the early years of the automobile, there were no drivers' licenses. There were no age limits for drivers. There was no auto insurance. This soon changed. Automobile owners had to register their cars. New York was the first state to give drivers' licenses to certain drivers. Then New Jersey drivers had to have a license to drive. They had to pass an exam to get a license.

The United States needed a road system. The Bureau of Public Roads was created in Washington, D.C. in 1915. It worked with the states to take care of and organize the roads. Old roads were repaired and new, paved ones were built. Lines were painted on the roads to mark traffic lanes. Speed limits were established. The limits were

Before World War II, the average American traveled no more than 50 miles from home during his or her lifetime.

posted on signs. Roads were given route numbers. Major highways received U.S. highway numbers. Routes that ran north to south were given odd numbers. Routes that ran east to west were given even numbers.

President Eisenhower knew there was a need for wide, smooth, well-marked highways. These highways must connect state-to-state and coast-to-coast. He was sure that this type of highway system would improve safety. It could help businesses and small towns grow.

The government created the U.S. Interstate Highway System in 1956. Engineers began working on these Interstate highways. They tested road materials. They studied bridge and road plans. They built roads that were the same all across the country.

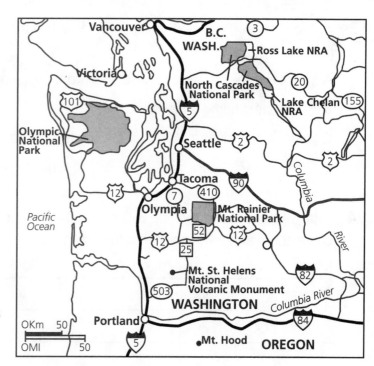

The U.S. Interstate Highway System was to be the largest project in U.S. history. It would take 40 years to build. It would have 54,000 bridges and 100 tunnels. More than 46,500 miles of Interstates would cross America. The roads would pass through every state in the nation.

1 Determine which of these *best* describes the overall structure of passage 1.

   A causes and effects

   B questions and answers

   C problems and solutions

   D sequence

2 Which of these *best* describes how the information in passage 2 is organized?

   A causes and effects

   B chronological order

   C compare and contrast

   D problems and solutions

3 In "Solving the Problems of America's Roads," the last paragraph
mainly _____.

    A explains the details of the solution to a problem

    B compares riding a bicycle to riding a horse

    C contrasts crossing a river by ferry with using a bridge

    D explains the cause and effect of not requiring drivers' licenses

4 Analyze the two passages. Explain why the authors of these passages
chose to organize their material the way they did.

_____

_____

_____

_____

_____

5 Evaluate how the overall organization is different in each passage.

_____

_____

_____

_____

_____

UNIT 3 ▨▨▨▨▨▨▨▨▨▨▨▨▨▨▨▨▨▨▨▨▨▨▨▨▨▨▨▨▨▨▨▨▨▨▨▨▨▨
Craft and Structure

Point of View and Author's Purpose

RL.4.6, RI.4.6

Vocabulary

creatures

dawning

embarrassing

haunting

panic

quill

routine

tunic

twilight

All writing has a *point of view.* In fiction, stories can be told from a character's point of view. They could also be told from a narrator's point of view. A poem is also told from the point of view of a speaker.

Nonfiction has a point of view, too. Imagine that you are reading a story about the pioneers going west. From the point of view of American history, settling the West was a good thing. A story written by a pioneer who lost his family on the trail would have a very different point of view. Native Americans would have a different point of view as well. Each story would be told in a different way. Each story would feel different to the reader. When you read, it is important to think about who tells the story. Think about *how* and *why* the story is told. When reading, it is important to know the point of view and author's purpose and how they influence what you are reading.

Point of View in Literary Text

When you read literary text, you have to ask one important question. Who is telling the story? In some stories, a character is the narrator. This is called the **first-person point of view.** You can tell if a story is written from a first-person point of view because the narrator uses the first-person pronouns *I* and *we.*

Many stories are told from a **third-person point of view.** The narrator uses pronouns like *he, she,* and *they.* A third-person narrator may take the point of view of one or more characters. Sometimes the third-person narrator is removed from the events and story. The narrator only observes and does not take sides with characters.

Guided Practice

Only the Moon and Stars

On the western horizon, the sunset signals
the sleeping of the sun, yellow and pink.
The last rays of light go home,
Twilight¹ brings the dawning² of the dark.

5 Day animals sleep in dreams,
Houses sit quiet, dark, and still.
In the blackness, the night comes alive,
And creatures³ of the dark awake.

Powdery moths and drawn to lamps,
10 They lightly tap on window screens.
Around the pond, bullfrogs call jug-o-rum, jug-o-rum,
While green frogs sing their high-pitched songs.

In grassy fields, crickets chirp,
Field mice sniff and snuffle,
15 Raccoons, busy bodies clunking,
Searching trash cans for their food.

Coyotes howl, calling out in the blackness,
Stray cats yowl, looking for their friends,
From a tree, the haunting⁴ owl watches
20 And asks hoo-hoo-hoo, hoo-hoo-who?

An acrobatic cloud of bats,
Storms silently across the sky.
Only the moon and stars linger,
As witnesses to the creatures of the night.

---

¹twilight: the faint light in the sky between sunset and darkness

²dawning: beginning to appear

³creatures: living things

⁴haunting: repeating

Analyze the poem. What is the point of view of this poem?

A first person

B third person, told by a speaker outside the poem

C third person, from the point of view of one animal

D third person, revealing the thoughts of several animals

The poem does not use first-person pronouns like *I*. Choice A is incorrect. The story tells about animals that are active during the night. The speaker is not expressing the point of view of one animal (choice C) or of several animals (choice D). The speaker observes and reports what a speaker outside the poem sees and hears. The correct answer is choice B.

Describe the events of the poem from your own point of view.

_____

_____

_____

_____

_____

You have read the poem. Your point of view about the poem is as important as anyone else's. Here is a sample answer:

When the sun sets and darkness falls, people, houses, and day animals go to sleep. While they are sleeping, night animals wake up. Moths, crickets, frogs, mice, raccoons, cats, coyotes, bats, and owls make noise. They search for food and call to one another. The moon and stars are the only ones awake to see them.

Point of View in Informational Text

Informational pieces have points of view, too. In writing about ideas or facts, the point of view is the author's. The author's purpose for writing tells more about her point of view. Two people writing about the same event or topic may have entirely different purposes. Both writers may have different points of view.

Think of a traffic accident report. A police officer comes to the scene. He has to write down what he observes. The police officer tries not to take sides. The report is meant to **inform** or **explain.**

Now, think about a traffic accident from the point of view of the driver that was hit. He may believe he did nothing wrong. He was the victim. He believes that it was the other person who caused the traffic accident. His report will try to **persuade** the reader that it was not his fault.

Imagine that you have just witnessed the traffic accident. You write an email to your friend telling her about the traffic accident you saw. You are most likely writing to **describe** what happened.

Guided Practice

Read two passages. Then answer the questions.

embarrassing
causing someone to feel self-conscious

Afraid of the Dark

Dear Diary,

I am afraid of the dark, and I am not afraid to say it out loud. I am afraid of the dark. I'm a sixth grade boy who is afraid of the dark. No, I don't think there are tigers or werewolves under my bed, and I am not scared of monsters or aliens in my closet. I am, and always have been, afraid of the dark. Please, just don't tell my friends.

When I was a very little kid, I was upset if I was left in the dark—even for just a few seconds. If I woke up in the middle of the night in the dark, I was terrified. It didn't matter if I was in the car, outdoors, or even in my own bed. I would scream and cry until someone turned on the light. Even now, if I wake up because I need to use the bathroom, I don't. I hold it until morning. The light switch is way across my room, and I'd never walk all the way down the hall in the dark. No way!

It gets more embarrassing as you get older. The summer before fourth grade, my friend Joe invited me to sleep out in his tent in the backyard. His mom and dad invited me to a cookout. His dad grilled hot dogs. His mom made us marshmallow and chocolate campfire treats. We played Frisbee with Joe's dog, Sam. Our camping gear was all set—we had sleeping bags, water bottles, flashlights, baseball cards, and joke books. However, as soon as the sun went down, I felt panic sinking in. Never mind the flashlight; I knew that it would be dark very soon. I started to panic. I really hated to seem like a wimp, but I had to tell Joe that I wasn't feeling very well. I had to go home.

panic
sudden fear for no reason

All these years, I have hated going out after dark. Now that I'm older, and I'm allowed to stay out later, it's worse. I have to think up lame excuses. It's humiliating. When it comes to trick-or-treating after dark with my friends, I have to say, "No thanks." Want to go to the fireworks on the Fourth of July? Nope. Want to go to the amusement park tomorrow night? No, I can't. I don't even like to go to the movie theater! Now that I think about it, I'm not too keen on winter either. By December, it gets dark before dinner, and it's still dark when I have to get up in the morning—gives me the creeps.

Sometimes I wonder if I'm going to be afraid of the dark for the rest of my life. Whenever I say something about it at home, my parents say "It's no big deal. You'll outgrow it. You'll get over it. Just you make up your mind about it."

I know from astronomy that the earth is dark for half of each day. That's half the time. I figured out that it means I've spent half of my life—five whole years—in the dark being afraid. That's not right, I tell you. It's just not fair!

Javier

Get Over It!

Your fear of the dark is all in your head. If you want to get over being afraid of the dark, you really need to put your mind to it. Then you can take some simple, common sense steps to face your fears and gradually overcome them.

Remember, there is nothing in the dark that can hurt you. In fact, you are probably safer in the dark than you are in the daylight. Have you ever thought about the difference between you and someone who is *not* afraid of the dark? Chances are the answer is *nothing.* Are you afraid of the dark, or are you afraid of what is *in* the dark? Maybe you fear monsters, snakes, spiders, werewolves, or aliens. Honestly, does that make sense? Of all the people in the world, why would they want to bother *you?* Believe it or not, you may be scaring yourself. If you are watching horror movies and reading scary books, it's time to stop. Give those violent computer games a rest. Turn off the crime show TV. Did you know that watching the news bothers some people so much they can't sleep?

It helps to admit your fears to yourself. Have that conversation and then talk about them with someone you can trust. It's good to talk through your feelings. Listen to someone else's experiences with their fears. You never know—maybe your dad was afraid of the vacuum cleaner when he was young! Write down the reasons you feel afraid. Think them through during the daylight hours.

Try to get used to the dark. Sit in a room with the lights on and look all around at everything. Then turn out the lights in the room. Practice spending short periods of time in the dark room. You may want to use a timer. Learn to be alone in the dark. Gradually increase the amount of time you spend in the dark. Prove to yourself that there is nothing to fear.

When my sister was young, she was afraid of the dark. She would practice opening the door to a dark room and shout, "I am not afraid of the dark!" Believe it or not, it worked! You don't need to shout, but talking yourself through it does help.

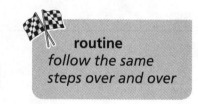

routine
follow the same steps over and over

If sleeping in a dark room is a problem, create a bedtime routine. Try to relax. Have a pleasant conversation. Laugh, read a good book, and think good thoughts. Pamper yourself. Check all your "scary places" before getting in bed. Then go to bed happy. Use a night lamp or keep the hall light on and your door open. Over time, close the door a little bit more each night.

Have faith. You can do it. In time, you might even learn to laugh at your fear of the dark.

Determine the point of view of "Afraid of the Dark."

A first person

B third person, told by a narrator outside the story

C third person, from the point of view of one character

D third person, revealing the thoughts of several characters

The 10-year-old boy uses the pronoun *I* as he talks to his diary. The passage is written from the first-person point of view. Choice A is the correct answer. A narrator or character is not telling the story. Choices B, C, and D are incorrect.

Describe how point of view influences "Afraid of the Dark."

_____

_____

_____

_____

_____

Here is a sample answer:

The narrator of "Afraid of the Dark" is a 10-year-old boy. Javier is writing about his own feelings in his diary. He is embarrassed about being afraid of the dark. His fear interferes with activities in his daily life. Javier is also worried that his friends will find out about his fear and tease him.

Which of these *best* expresses the author's point of view in "Get Over It"?

A It's all in your head.

B Fear of the dark is impossible to overcome.

C Computer games are bad for you.

D Don't tell anyone that you are afraid of the dark.

> The author does not say that it is impossible to overcome a fear of the dark. He does not comment on whether computer games are a bad influence. The author does not say that you should keep your fears to yourself. Choices B, C, and D are incorrect. He thinks that fear of the dark is all in your head, and you can learn how to overcome it. Choice A is the correct answer.

Compare and contrast the point of views and authors' purposes for writing "Afraid of the Dark" and "Get Over It."

_____

_____

_____

_____

_____

_____

_____

> Analyze the two passages. How are they the same? How are they different? Here is a sample answer:

The two authors are writing on the same topic. Yet, the passages each have a different purpose. In "Afraid of the Dark," a young boy writes about his fear of the dark and how he feels about this. The passage has a serious tone. The passage is written in the first person. In contrast, the author of "Get Over It" is not afraid of the dark. The author explains why people should not be afraid of the dark. He also offers some advice on overcoming this fear. He also jokes about it. This passage is also written in the first person.

Test Yourself

Laetitia and the Redcoats

adapted from the 1889 short story by Lillian L. Price

Laetitia burst through her grandparents' door pulling her hood off her curls. With great pains she said, "Neighbor Paxton just told me something awful. Oh, Grandmother, the British are crossing the valley. Master Paxton says they will camp here at nightfall! He says you and Grandfather must depart at once."

"Calm thyself, Laetitia. For these troubled times are not for the children and old. We have strong men that are fighting for us. You must be brave." Grandfather looked Laetitia squarely in the face. "We will move the family to the mountain until they leave."

"I will then, Grandfather. Not a tear will I shed." After she spoke, she wandered through her grandparents' home, a house she loved dearly. She could not imagine British soldiers clanking about the house. Her eyes filled with soft tears. Out of the corner of her watery eye, she saw pen and ink. Just then she had an idea. The quill was new and the ink was good.

Slowly and thoughtfully the little fingers guided the quill along the faint lines. First, across one sheet she wrote and then across the other:

quill
hollow shaft of a feather used to write with when dipped in ink

To THE REDCOATS:

I am Laetitia Wright, aged 14, who lives in this house with my grandparents. They are old and feeble folk, gentle and peaceful to friend and foe. I pray you, dear Redcoats, spare their home to them, and do not burn nor ruin our house. Perhaps thou hast a little maid like me in England, and old parents. Thou couldst not burn the roof from over their heads, and in such pity and mercy, spare ours! We leave thee much to eat, and would leave thee more, were our store larger.

Signed, LAETITIA WRIGHT

Before she and her grandparents left for the safety of the mountain, Laetitia put the letter in the door knocker. After they reached safety, the British soldiers came to their town and occupied their home. One of the officers found Laetitia's letter, and it brought tears to his eyes. How bold this little girl is to write such a letter, he thought. We shall not destroy anything in this town.

A few days later, the bugles blew. This let the folks on the mountain know it was safe to come back to their homes. When Laetitia arrived home, she found a note from a British soldier.

"Sweet Mistress Wright, we bid you good-night,
'Tis time for us soldiers to wander.
We've paid for your geese, a penny apiece,
And left the change with the gander.
Though redcoats we be, you plainly will see,
We know how to grant a petition.
With rough solider care, we've endeavored to spare
Your homes in a decent condition."

The letter was signed by the colonel and by a number of soldiers. When Laetitia told her grandparents what she had done, they kissed and thanked her.

The Redcoats Are Coming!

Do you hear the cry of Paul Revere? These words remind us of a great American Revolutionary War legend. Patriot Paul Revere waited for a lantern signal in the steeple of Old North Church. One lantern meant the enemy had come by land. The English had come by horseback or had walked into Boston. Two lanterns meant the British had come by sea. They had come by boat or on ships. When Paul Revere saw the signal, he rode his horse through the streets of Boston. He cried out to warn the people, "The Redcoats are coming!"

Have you ever wondered why English soldiers were nicknamed the "Redcoats"? It is more legend than fact. Stories and legends about early America use the term "Redcoats." Some say that the people of Boston called English soldiers "lobster backs." However, very old records show that they were really called "Regulars" or "the King's men." In fact, it was not until one hundred years later that the name "Redcoat" was commonly used. Today, it is not considered polite to use this term.

You may wonder why the English wore red coats. Red does seem like a risky color to wear in battle. Red coats made English soldiers easier to spot. It was hard to hide in those bright red coats! However, those coats did not stay bright red for long. Uniforms were made of wool. The wool was dipped in cheap vegetable dye to give it color. Vegetable dyes faded quickly. The longer the coats were worn, the more they faded. Hot weather made them fade even faster. The coats turned pink or reddish-brown.

British soldiers have always worn uniforms with red coats or scarlet tunics. In 1645, the red coat became part of the official uniform of the English military. Some coats were red and white. Some were red and gold, the colors of the royal family. Red is the national color of Great Britain. Today, most British military dress uniforms include very bright red coats. They are worn in parades and special events.

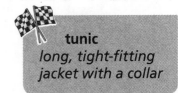

tunic
long, tight-fitting jacket with a collar

1 Determine the point of view used in "Laetitia and the Redcoats."

   A first person

   B third person, told by a narrator outside the story

   C third person, from the point of view of one character

   D third person, revealing the thoughts of several characters

2 What is the point of view of "The Redcoats Are Coming!"?

   A first person

   B third person, told by a narrator outside the story

   C third person, from the point of view of one character

   D third person, revealing the thoughts of several characters

3 In "Laetitia and the Redcoats," how does the narrator's point of view influence the tone of her letter to the Redcoats?

_____

_____

_____

_____

_____

4 What is the author's purpose in writing the passage "The Redcoats Are Coming!"?

_____

_____

_____

_____

_____

5 The author of "The Redcoats Are Coming!" says that the word "Redcoats" was never really used until one hundred years after the Revolutionary War. Yet, Lillian L. Price uses the word "Redcoats" in her story, "Laetitia and the Redcoats." Explain this difference in the authors' point of views.

_____

_____

_____

_____

_____

UNIT 3 ❌❌❌❌❌❌❌❌❌❌❌❌❌❌❌❌❌❌❌❌❌❌❌❌❌❌
Craft and Structure

REVIEW

Craft and Structure

Vocabulary

chrysalis
cuisine
culture
edible
harvested
molt
pesticides
snatched

snatched
reached or grabbed

Read the passages. Then answer the questions.

The Legend of the Butterflies

a Papago legend

Part 1

One day as the Creator was sitting and resting, he watched some children at play in a village. The children laughed and sang, but as he watched them, his heart was sad. He thought, "These children will grow old. Their skin will become wrinkled, their hair will turn gray, and the young hunter's arm will weaken. The playful puppies will become old mangy dogs. And those wonderful flowers— yellow and blue, red and purple—will fade, and the leaves from the trees will fall and dry up. Already they are turning yellow." The Creator grew sadder and sadder. It was autumn, and he thought of the coming winter. Winter is bitter and cold; nothing is green. Thinking about it made his heart heavy.

Yet, it was still warm, and the sun was shining. The Creator watched the play of sunlight and shadows on the ground. The yellow leaves blew here and there in the brisk wind. The Creator saw the blueness of the sky. He saw the whiteness of the cornmeal some women had spilled on the ground. Suddenly he smiled. "All those vibrant colors must be saved. I'll make something extraordinary that will make my heart sing—something for these children to look at and enjoy forever," he thought.

The Creator took out his bag and started gathering colorful things. He caught a spot of sunlight, and he snatched a handful of blue from the sky. He picked up the whiteness of the cornmeal, and he collected the shadows of playing children. He pulled the blackness of a beautiful girl's hair. He grabbed the yellow of the falling leaves, and he reached for the green of the pine needles. He gathered the red, purple, and orange from the flowers around him. He even gathered the song of the songbird. All these he put into his bag.

1 Which of these *best* describes this passage?

   A a play

   B a folk song

   C a story

   D a poem

2 What is the point of view of this passage?

   A first person

   B third person, told by a narrator outside the story

   C third person, from the point of view of one character

   D third person, revealing the thoughts of several characters

3 Read this line from the passage.

   Winter is bitter and cold; nothing is green.

  How does this relate to the Creator's point of view about the children?

   A The Creator doesn't like winter or children.

   B The Creator likes winter and he knows that the children also like it.

   C The Creator is sad that the children are young and sad that winter is coming.

   D The Creator is thinking about the children growing old and winter symbolizes old age.

4 How does the structure of the story make the reader want to continue reading?

   A It makes the reader wonder what is in the bag.

   B It makes the reader wonder if the children get old.

   C It makes the reader question why Creator is sad.

   D It makes the reader question the unfairness of life and aging.

UNIT 3 ✖✖✖✖✖✖✖✖✖✖✖✖✖✖✖✖✖✖✖✖✖✖✖✖✖✖✖✖✖✖✖✖✖✖✖✖
Craft and Structure

The Legend of the Butterflies

Part 2

CREATOR *(walking to an open grassy area):* Children, little children! I've created this special gift for you.

The Creator gives the children his bag.

CREATOR: Open it, children. There's something extraordinary inside.

CHILDREN *(opening bag):* Look, it's hundreds of beautiful flying creatures filled with every color. What are they?

CREATOR: They are butterflies. They are my new creation so that you may enjoy and dance with them.

CHILDREN: Look how they dance in our hair. They flutter. They are singing so beautifully.

CREATOR: Yes, they sip nectar from the flowers and they dance around singing the songs so beautiful about the flowers.

CHILDREN: We have never seen anything so beautiful. Let us listen to them.

Songbird flies out from nowhere and settles on the Creator's shoulder.

CREATOR: Well, hello songbird. Meet the butterflies.

SONGBIRD: It is not right that you give our songs to these new, pretty creations. When you made us, you told us that every bird would have his own song. Now you have given our beautiful songs away. Is it not enough that you gave the butterflies all of the colors of the rainbow?

CREATOR: You are right. I made one special song for each bird. I should not take away what belongs to you.

CHILDREN: The butterfly is silent now. But it is just as beautiful with or without a voice.

5 The two passages could *best* be described as _____.

  A a folk song and a poem

  B a poem and a play

  C a fairy tale and a poem

  D a legend and a play

6 How are the children's and the songbird's point of view about the butterflies different?

    A The children are jealous of the butterflies and the songbird is excited by them.

    B The children are excited by the butterflies and the songbird is happy about them.

    C The children are no longer lonely and the songbird is no longer sad.

    D The children are delighted with the butterflies and the songbird is jealous of them.

7 Briefly retell Part 2 of the story from the songbird's point of view.

_____

_____

_____

_____

8 The author's purpose in writing is to _____.

    A inform

    B entertain

    C describe

    D persuade

9 How do the events in Part 2 of the story build on the events in Part 1?

_____

_____

_____

_____

UNIT 3
Craft and Structure

Passage 1

Insect Life Cycles

Insects are the largest class of animals in the world. Flying, crawling, creeping, and wriggling insects are everywhere. To understand how insects live, we need to understand how they grow and change during the stages in their life cycles.

Egg–Adult

The lives of all insects are divided into stages. Some insects go through many stages during their life cycles. Other insects go through only one stage. Insects without wings are an example of an insect with a one-stage life cycle. Silverfish fall into this group. They hatch from *eggs* as small adults. Then they grow larger into *adults*. There are only a small number of insects that have a one-stage life cycle. Most insects go through more than one stage.

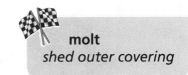

molt
shed outer covering

Egg–Nymph–Adult

Sometimes insects go through two stages in their life cycle. Grasshoppers and dragonflies are examples of this type of insect. They look like small adults when they hatch from their *eggs*. However, their wings and other body parts are not mature. These insects are in the *nymph* stage. Nymphs molt or shed their skin again and again. Slowly, they become *adults*. These insects may lose extra body parts, such as extra legs, as they molt. Some nymphs live on land. Some nymphs live in water.

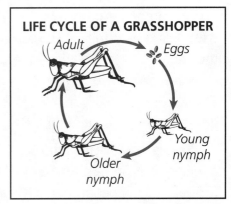

LIFE CYCLE OF A GRASSHOPPER

Egg–Larva–Pupa–Adult

Insects that go through three stages before becoming an adult are the most common. These include butterflies, moths, beetles, and flies. These insects begin life as *eggs*. The eggs hatch into *larva*.

Caterpillars, grubs, and maggots are the larvae stages of butterflies, beetles, and flies. Larvae are always hungry. They eat all the time. It is their job to grow. When insect larvae reach their full size, they stop eating.

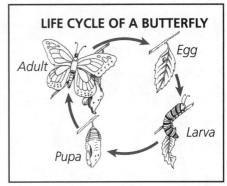

LIFE CYCLE OF A BUTTERFLY

The insects then begin the resting stage. Now, they are called a *pupa*. The insects form a chrysalis. This protects them. Inside the chrysalis, the larva changes into an *adult* insect. If you have ever been lucky enough to watch a butterfly emerge from its chrysalis, you know the wonder and beauty of the insect world.

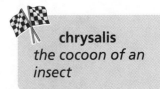

chrysalis
the cocoon of an insect

Would You Like Bugs with That?

People learn what foods to eat from their family. Friends and communities eat certain foods. Our ideas and feelings about food depend on where we grow up. Our culture is much more important than how edible a food is.

People from America, Canada, and Europe cannot imagine eating insects. Finding an insect cookbook would be hard. Finding a restaurant with insects on the menu would be even harder.

To us, the idea of insects on a plate is horrible. We think biting into a crunchy insect in a salad would be awful! We have not been taught to eat insects. In some places of the world, however, people think that eating honey, milk, or cheese is disgusting! Yet, they may have no problem eating a snack of roasted termites.

All over the world, people eat insects. They are part of people's normal diet. In all, people eat about 500 different kinds of insects. The most common ones are grasshoppers, crickets, termites, bees, wasps, and caterpillars. Humans have been eating insects for thousands of years. Native Americans used insects as part of their diet. Grasshoppers were a favorite food. They would collect grasshoppers. Then they would dry or roast them. They would eat them whole or grind them up to put in bread.

In Asia, some restaurants serve boiled baby wasps, fried grasshoppers, or caterpillars. In East Africa, termites are a great treat. In food markets in South Africa, people can buy caterpillars. They are a special treat. In Australia, the native people bite the bellies off honey pot ants. They have sweet liquid inside. They taste like candy. In South America, you can buy bags of roasted ants at the movie theater. People eat them like popcorn.

These insects are good for you. They are a healthy food choice. They are high in proteins, vitamins, and minerals. They are low in bad fats.

How about it? Wouldn't you love to tickle your taste buds with some creepy, crawly lean cuisine?

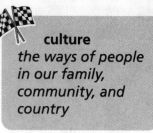

culture
the ways of people in our family, community, and country

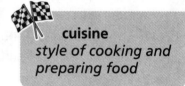

edible
fit to be eaten

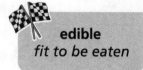

cuisine
style of cooking and preparing food

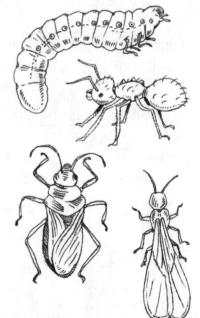

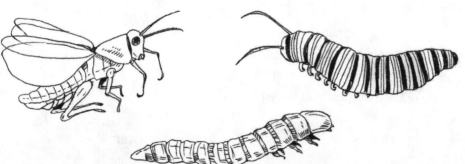

Dear Editors:

I just read the article in your newspaper about our food supply in America. I am writing to tell you that I am not happy that there are insects in my food. I never knew that I was eating bugs all the time.

I didn't know that when crops are harvested, some insects get harvested, too. Some insects or insect parts get mixed in when food is being made. I have found bugs in fresh fruits and vegetables. I hate when that happens, but it's pretty normal. I did not know that there are bees' legs and bee hairs in the honey. There are even tiny insect larvae in flour and pasta. Worst of all, there are teeny-tiny bugs in spices—so tiny you can't see them.

Then I read that the U. S. Food and Drug Administration allows some insect parts in our food. Does the president know about this? Will he continue to eat cereal for breakfast? Will he eat honey? I know that I will not anymore.

Bugs in food should not happen in America! The solution is simple. We should have more pesticides on our food to keep the bugs out!

Thank you,

Julie Greene

harvested
brought in or gathered crops

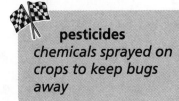

pesticides
chemicals sprayed on crops to keep bugs away

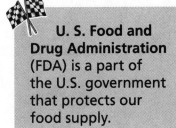

U. S. Food and Drug Administration (FDA) is a part of the U.S. government that protects our food supply.

10 How is the information in passage 1 organized?

A as a comparison of insect life cycles

B as a series of causes and effects

C as a series of questions and answers

D as a series of problems and solutions

11 The information in passage 2 is mainly presented _____.

A in chronological order

B as a series of causes and effects

C in order of importance, from greatest to least

D as a comparison and contrast of two environments

12 The author of passage 3 organizes the information ____.

    A in no particular order

    B as cause and effect

    C as a problem and solution

    D in chronological order or sequence

13 The authors of all three passages would agree that ____.

    A insects have a role in all of our lives

    B life-cycles of insects have two or more stages

    C our attitudes toward eating insects depend on our culture.

    D insects are a tasty and healthy food choice.

14 Compare the point of view for passage 2 and passage 3. Fill in the graphic organizer to answer the questions about the author's point of view of each passage.

Passage 2	Author's Point of View	Passage 3
	Why did the author write this passage? (author's purpose)	
	To whom is the author writing?	
	What was the author's tone or mood?	
	How did the author present her facts, opinions, and ideas?	

Craft and Structure

Integration of Knowledge and Ideas

The information you read comes from many sources. Reading more than one text about the same subject can help you. It can tell you whether or not the information you are reading is true.

When you read stories, you can also compare characters. This helps you understand what is the same and what is different about people. This also helps you understand that the same kind of stories can be told in different ways.

Pictures can also help you deepen your understanding. When you compare texts and pictures, you can enjoy your reading and get more out of it. You can also make different connections. You can ask yourself what is the same about the texts and pictures you read. Then you could ask yourself what is different.

This unit is all about how you take in ideas from your reading. It is about how you combine this information. And it is about how you make new ideas from all this.

- **In Lesson 11,** you will learn how pictures can add meaning to texts. You'll also learn how reading more than one text on the same topic can help you answer questions.

- **Lesson 12** is about what you read in your texts. You'll learn how to tell whether or not the facts you read can be proven. In other words, you'll learn how to tell if the information you're reading is true.

- **In Lesson 13,** you will learn to compare texts. You will note what is similar and different about them. You can use this knowledge to help you understand what you read.

Visual Literacy

RI.4.7

Vocabulary

consistent

crystalline rock

intensity

plateau

sedimentary rock

summit

Have you ever heard anyone say, "A picture is worth a thousand words"? This is true of other visual elements as well. Photographs, charts, graphs, and maps enhance what you are reading. Illustrations and diagrams can give you a better understanding of complex material. All of these can bring a deeper meaning to what you are reading.

Guided Practice

Read the passage. Then answer the questions.

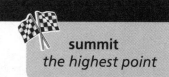

summit
the highest point

Climbing Mount Everest

by Catherine Bevard

Do you know what the highest point in the world is? It is Mount Everest. The peak of the mountain is 29,035 feet high. In the 1990s, people started using tools to track changes on it. The tools have shown us that the mountain moves a little bit to the northeast every year. It also rises a fraction of an inch each year. So, the world's highest point keeps getting even higher.

It took a long time for anyone to climb to the top of Mount Everest. In 1953, two men made it to the top. In 1980, the first person climbed to the mountain's top alone. In 2001, a blind man made it to the mountain's peak. In 2010, the world was shocked when Jordan Romero, age 13, made it to the mountain's summit. He is the youngest person to climb the mountain.

Jordan Romero and Ang Pasang, a Sherpa guide, reach the summit of Mount Everest.

UNIT 4 ▨▨▨▨▨▨▨▨▨▨▨▨▨▨▨▨▨▨▨▨▨▨▨▨
Integration of Knowledge and Ideas

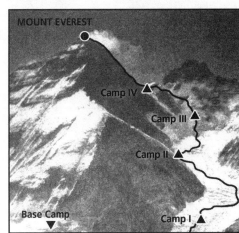

There is a reason that few people reach the top of the mountain. It is a challenge in many ways. First, the weather on the mountain is so harsh that it cannot support human life. The weather is not the only issue. The mountain is so high that a climber's pulse and heart rate go up as his body works harder to get enough oxygen. Many climbers bring extra oxygen with them for the climb. Some try to finish the climb without it.

There are a few routes to the top that people can take when they climb the mountain. The south route is the most common. The north path is used less, but people still climb it sometimes. People do not climb the East Face, the mountain's biggest side, very much. Whatever path these climbers take, trying to reach the top of Mount Everest is dangerous. Yet, many still make it one of their life goals to reach the mountain's summit.

Which of these facts is *best* illustrated by the trail map above?

A The weather on Mount Everest is very harsh.

B There are no humans living on Mount Everest.

C Mount Everest is so high that climbers need camps at which to rest on their way up the mountain.

D Many climbers bring extra oxygen with them when climbing Mount Everest.

Not only can you see what Mount Everest looks like, but you can also see the location of many camps for the tired climbers. Also, you can see a black line showing you the mountain trail that climbers can take to reach the summit. These camps are along that trail. Choice C is the correct answer. The map does not show that the weather is harsh or that there aren't any people living on Mount Everest. It also does not show that climbers bring extra oxygen with them because the air is so thin.

How does the trail map of Mount Everest add meaning to the information in the article you read?

_____

_____

_____

_____

 Maps can add to our knowledge and understanding. This map provides additional information not mentioned in the passage. Here is a sample answer:

> The article explains why climbing Mount Everest is hard. It describes different challenges that people will face when climbing it. The map shows the trail that the people have to climb to reach the top. It also shows camps along the way. These camps are not mentioned in the article.

The photograph of Jordan Romero on page 152 can help you understand

_____.

A how high Mount Everest truly is

B how thin the air is on Mount Everest

C that Mount Everest was named after Sir George Everest

D that Sherpas live in the valleys below Mount Everest

 The passage can tell you how how harsh the conditions are, but a photograph gives you a very good idea of this by the way the climbers are dressed and what gear they have. Did you notice that Jordan and his guide have oxygen masks connected to oxygen canisters? This can help you understand how thin the air is on Mount Everest. Choice A is the correct answer.

Using information from the article, determine what you think Jordan needed to have when climbing Mount Everest.

_____

_____

_____

_____

 You need to use information from both the photograph and the passage to answer this. Here is a sample answer:

In the article, you learn that the conditions are harsh. The photograph of Jordan shows that he needed extremely warm clothing, googles, extra oxygen, and climbing gear. He also climbed with a Sherpa guide, named Ang Pasang, who knew the trail to the summit.

Read the passage. Then answer the questions.

How Mountains Are Formed

by Catherine Bevard

sedimentary rock
rock formed by mineral and organic matter

You have seen photographs of mountains. You might have even visited mountains before. Do you know how mountains are formed? Do you know how they became so large, and where they came from?

Mountains are formed when Earth's plates fold, unfold, and collide with each other. They can also be formed by volcanic rock. The Himalayan Mountains were formed when one plate pressed against each other. The Earth's crust folded, causing the land to rise. Other mountains have been created when one plate sinks below another plate.

How can you be sure that what you see is a mountain, and not a hill or a plateau? Mountains stand very high above the land around them. Their sides are usually very steep.

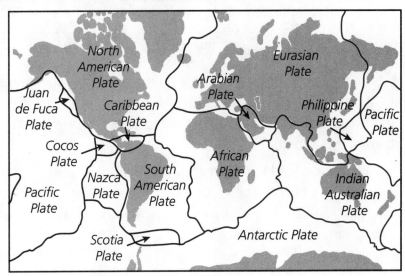
Earth's plates

Plateaus have sloping sides. The tops of mountains form peaks that are much smaller than the mountain's base. Plateaus have a flat area above the surrounding land. They are found alone. Most mountains do not stand alone. They are usually found in ranges or chains. The mountains that make up these chains are joined by ridges and separated by valleys. When many of these ranges or chains are found together, they are called a "mountain belt." Mountain belts are very large. They are usually ten to hundreds of kilometers wide.

When sedimentary rock folds and creates layers, fold belts occur. Often, these fold belts include areas where older rocks push up and and over younger rocks. When this happens, the belt is called a "thrust and fold belt." When crystalline rocks push against each other, the thrust creates higher mountains. The Himalayas are the biggest mountains in the world. They were created by this sort of thrust.

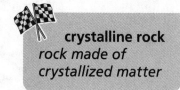

plateau
land area raised above the earth, with a flat top

crystalline rock
rock made of crystallized matter

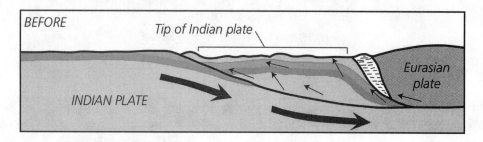

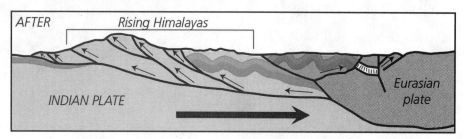

The Himalayan Mountains formed when the Indian plate pressed against the Eurasian plate. Then part of Earth's crust folded over another crust.

All mountain belts have some differences. They also have things in common. Their similarities allow Earth scientists to put them into different groups. Each group is created based on the process that made the mountain belt.

Wind, rain, and ice all wear away mountains. Parts of them crumble and fall off. These parts become soil, sand, and sediment. Because of their large size, though, the mountains can withstand a lot of wear and still stand tall.

Compare the two passages. Which of these facts is found in "Climbing Mount Everest," but *not* in "How Mountains Are Formed"?

A The Himalayas are the biggest mountains in the world.

B Jordan Romero climbed Mount Everest when he was 13 years old.

C Fold belts happen when sedimentary rock creates layers.

D Some mountains were formed by tectonic plates pressing against each other.

Sometimes when you read two similar texts you will find the same information in both. However, you will also find that some facts are given in only one of the readings. "How Mountains Are Formed" explained how mountains are formed. It did not tell about those who have climbed these mountains. "Climbing Mount Everest" discussed mountain climbers, including Jordan. The passage tells that he climbed Mount Everest when he was 13, making him the youngest person to climb the mountain. Choice B is the correct answer.

What do the illustrations in "How Mountains Are Formed" show?

_____

_____

Illustrations can help you better understand concepts discussed in a text. Here is a sample answer:

The map shows the location of the Earth's plates. The diagrams show how the Himalayas were formed.

Evaluate what you have learned about a plateau and a mountain. What is similar about a plateau and a mountain? How are they different?

_____

_____

_____

✓ This question asks you to compare and contrast information. Here is a sample answer:

> Both are raised areas of land. However, plateaus are flat on top, while mountains have smaller peaks. Also, plateaus are more likely to stand by themselves. Mountains are usually found in ranges.

Imagine that your teacher has asked you to write a report about mountains. List four facts from both texts and their visual aids that you might include.

_____

_____

_____

_____

✓ If you were writing a report on the topic, you would combine information from several sources. Including information from text and visual elements can help you. You could answer a question or solve a problem better when you use more than one source. Here is a sample answer:

> 1—The first people to climb Mount Everest did so in 1953.
> 2—Jordan Romero climbed Mount Everest at the age of 13.
> 3—The Himalayas are the largest mountains in the world.
> 4—Ice, rain, and wind wear away at the mountains.

UNIT 4 ░░░
Integration of Knowledge and Ideas

Test Yourself

Passage 1

Solar Energy

Did you know that the sun can be used for energy? The sun is the biggest source of energy Earth receives. However, by the time the sunlight reaches Earth, it loses intensity. People had to find a way to store and use the sun's energy. Solar panels are one way to do this.

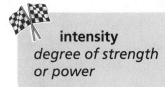

intensity
degree of strength or power

"Flat-plate collectors" are used to store sunlight and use it as energy. These are made of a metal plate and sheets of glass. The glass heats up when the sun shines on it. The heat then becomes air or water, which flows past the back of the plate. This heat can be used to heat homes or water.

Solar radiation can be turned into electricity. This is done by using solar cells. These cells convert the sun's heat and light into electricity. If only one cell is used, only about two watts of electricity is created. In solar panels, one can use many cells, and hundreds or thousands of kilowatts can be made.

Solar power has been used to power small things like watches and calculators. It has also been used in remote areas to power water pumps. Some countries use solar power for cooking.

While the sun's energy could be used for many things, it is expensive. Until the cost of generating and using it goes down, its use will stay limited.

Wind Power

Have you ever seen a wind turbine? Well, if you have ever seen what looks like a giant, white windmill, you have! These wind turbines are used to turn the wind into energy that people can use. In the past, windmills were used to grind grain. Now, wind power can be used to generate electricity!

Big wind turbines can have narrow blades that are up to 140 feet long. These blades can be placed on towers that are up to 280 feet tall! Turbines of this size are used to generate large amounts of power. Small turbines can be used to provide power to homes. In both turbines, the blades are made to capture the wind's energy and then convert it into another type of energy that people can use. Sometimes many wind turbines are placed together to create wind farms. These wind farms generate large amounts of power.

By the early 2000s, wind power was being used for 1% of the world's electricity. Using wind energy is not much more expensive than other forms of energy. It is also a renewable resource. This means it can replace itself over and over again.

Wind energy is not perfect, though. Wind is not a consistent source of energy. Wind turbines work best in areas with a lot of strong winds. Also, wind farms require large areas of land. There are concerns that this land will not be available for farming or ranching. People also worry that the wind farms will affect wildlife habitats.

Yet, there are many good things about wind energy. Wind energy does not produce waste, and it is a good way to generate power to small areas.

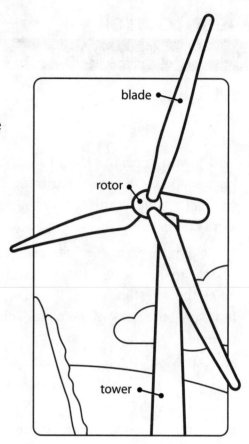

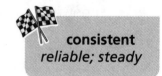

consistent
reliable; steady

1 In passage 1, which of these sentences is *best* illustrated by the photograph on page 159?

    A "Flat-plate" collectors are used to store sunlight and use it as energy.

    B While the sun's energy could be used for many things, it is expensive.

    C Solar power has been used to power small things like watches and calculators.

    D The sun is the biggest source of energy Earth receives.

2 In passage 1, how does the photograph on page 159 help your understanding of the passage?

_____

_____

_____

_____

3 What is one of the *main* concerns about solar energy?

    A It is wasteful.

    B We will run out of it.

    C The cost of keeping and using it.

    D There is no way to store the energy.

4 What is the purpose of the diagram on page 160 used to illustrate passage 2?

_____

_____

_____

_____

5 List three good things about wind energy.

_____

_____

_____

_____

_____

6 Why is it hard to use solar or wind energy to provide power to large areas?

_____

_____

_____

_____

_____

7 Evaluate the photographs used to illustrate passage 1 and passage 2. What can you conclude about the number of wind turbines or solar panels needed to generate energy?

_____

_____

_____

_____

_____

UNIT 4 ▓▓▓▓▓▓▓▓▓▓▓▓▓▓▓▓▓▓▓▓▓▓▓▓▓▓▓▓▓▓▓▓▓▓
Integration of Knowledge and Ideas

Identifying Connections

RI.4.8

When you read, do you know whether you are reading a factual account or someone's opinion? When you read, you need to understand the difference. A **fact** is a something that you can *prove*. An **opinion** tells you how someone *feels*. Look for words like *best* or *worst*. These words can mean the author is giving an opinion. Words like *always* and *never* often show opinions, too.

In some texts, you know the author is giving his opinion. Examples of these texts are book reviews and editorials. Sometimes, however, writers want you to agree with their position. They write to persuade you of a particular opinion. However, they should support their position or opinion with facts.

As you read, pay attention to what the author says. Does she write information that you can prove? Does it sound like the author knows what she is talking about? Is the author leaving out facts that don't support her opinions? Is the information current? Does the author present both sides of her story?

Ask yourself questions like these as you read. They will help you separate fact from opinion.

Guided Practice

Read the passage. Then answer the questions.

Susan's Recycling News

Tips You Can Use!

landfills
areas where trash and garbage are buried to build up low lying land

There are so many good things about recycling. Many people only think about the benefits to the environment, but the benefits don't stop there. Recycling can save money. Recycling items is less expensive than throwing them away. There is a cost to having landfills and picking up trash. When more people recycle, the cheaper it is to recycle. Recycling creates jobs. In fact, recycling has created more than a million of them!

Recycling is good for the earth, too. Every ton of paper that is recycled saves 17 trees! The more we recycle, the less pollution Earth will have.

We could do a lot better with our recycling. There are easy ways to do this. There is more to recycling than just putting cans in a recycling bin! When you go to the store, do you use paper bags? Do you use plastic bags? The best bags to use when you shop are cloth bags. These bags can be used over and over.

Other items also can be reused! Bottles and plastics can be recycled in bins to be used again, of course. You can give old clothes to charity, and you can buy used items instead of new ones. That way, items are getting another life instead of being sent to a landfill.

There are too many good things about recycling for anyone not to do it. Recycling saves energy. It saves natural resources. If we recycle more, we will need less land for landfills.

Some progress has been made. Since 1977, 2-liter soda bottles have gotten lighter, so less plastic is being used to make them. Because of that, we have saved 250 million pounds of plastic! Isn't that amazing?

Many people say that it is too hard to recycle. They do not think it is convenient. I think the facts speak for themselves. Everyone should recycle as much as possible. It makes too much sense not to.

What is the *main* point that Susan makes?

_____

_____

_____

 Here is a sample answer:

    Susan thinks that everyone should recycle because it is good for the environment and it conserves natural resources. This is her opinion. She tries to support her opinion with facts.

Integration of Knowledge and Ideas

Which sentence from paragraph 5 is an opinion?

A There are too many good things about recycling for anyone not to do it.

B Recycling saves energy.

C Recycling saves natural resources.

D If we recycle more, we will need less land for landfills.

Who decides how many things are "too many"? The other choices can be proven. However, you cannot prove how many things are "too many." This is the author's opinion. Many times you can spot an opinion by a writer's use of words. If there are words such as *best, worst, most, everyone,* and *nobody,* chances are there is an opinion given. Choice A is the right answer.

List two facts that Susan uses to support her main argument.

_____

_____

_____

_____

Often, facts will include numbers and dates that could be proven. This is called data, or research. Susan gives two data facts. Here is a sample answer:

1—Since 1977, 2-liter soda bottles have gotten lighter, so less plastic is being used.

2—We have saved 250 million pounds of plastic—and—every ton of paper that is recycled saves 17 trees!

Does Susan present both sides of the argument? Explain why, or why not.

_____

_____

_____

_____

✓ Analyze Susan's argument. Does she present only her opinion? Here is a sample answer:

Susan mainly presents her side. She does bring up opposing views. She explains that some people think it is not convenient to recycle. However, she mainly supports her argument that people should recycle.

Do you think Susan's closing paragraph helps convince the reader? Explain why, or why not.

_____

_____

_____

_____

✓ Susan has given some good reasons to recycle in her argument. Does she continue to do this in the last paragraph? Here is a sample answer:

Susan's last paragraph does convince the reader. She presents the other side of the argument. But then she mentions facts to support her side. The facts stand out. And she uses them well to help support her view.

UNIT 4 ▓▓▓▓▓▓▓▓▓▓▓▓▓▓▓▓▓▓▓▓▓▓▓▓▓▓▓▓▓▓▓▓▓▓▓▓
Integration of Knowledge and Ideas

Test Yourself

Dear Mr. Davis,

I am a fourth grader here at Washington Elementary School. I have a suggestion. I think that we should have a "Teacher of the Month" award. My teacher, Mrs. Johnson, should be the first one to receive this award.

Mrs. Johnson is a great teacher. She has a very special way of making everyone feel like her favorite. Whenever I have a problem, Mrs. Johnson is there for me. Sometimes, I think math is pretty hard, and Mrs. Johnson is never too busy to help me make sense of it. She also has a way of making it fun!

Last month, we got a new student in our classroom. His name is Toby. Toby moved here from out of town, and he did not know anyone. Mrs. Johnson welcomed him as if she had known him for a long time! She told us we would all have a new friend, and she helped us all get to know him better. I know Toby really felt better after the warm welcome he received.

Mrs. Johnson always seems to find a way to make things fun and educational. Sometimes, she has us play games, and at the end of the game, we realize we were learning things while we played. She helps us understand why it is important to get a good education, why it is important to pay attention in class, and why it is important to learn as much as we can.

When we're in Mrs. Johnson's classroom, we all feel very comfortable and safe. We know that she is looking out for all of us, and we know that she puts us first, always! She makes sure we understand everything she says, and she makes sure that everyone feels good about himself.

I know that we have a lot of good teachers here at Washington. I will probably have great teachers every year, which is why I think we should give this award every month! A lot of schools give awards like this. The students could vote for a different teacher every month. It would be nice for teachers to know that they are appreciated.

I hope you will consider letting us have this award. I know that Mrs. Johnson would be so happy. Other teachers would be happy to get the award, too.

Thank you for reading this, Mr. Davis. Maybe we could also have a principal's award!

Sincerely,

Becky Brown

1 What is the *main* point of Becky's letter?

_____

_____

_____

_____

2 What are three reasons Becky gives in support of her argument, and the evidence for each?

Reason a: _____

_____

Reason b: _____

_____

Reason c: _____

_____

3 Which of these sentences states an opinion?

   A Whenever I have a problem, Mrs. Johnson is there for me.

   B Last month, we got a new student in our classroom.

   C A lot of schools give awards like this.

   D She also has a way of making it fun!

UNIT 4
Integration of Knowledge and Ideas

4 Which of these sentences states a fact?

    A Last month, we got a new student in our classroom.

    B We should have a "Teacher of the Month" award.

    C It would be nice for teachers to know that they are appreciated.

    D My teacher, Mrs. Johnson, should be the first one to receive that award.

5 What is a point Becky makes that is *not* supported by reasons and evidence? Explain your answer.

_____

_____

_____

_____

_____

13

Comparing and Contrasting

RL.4.9, RI.4.9

Vocabulary

epidermis

humble

immortal

vaccine

What is your favorite type of story to read? The more you read, the more you see different themes in your texts. But what is a **theme?** A theme is a clear, unified idea in a story. Sometimes, you will find the theme in a story's **moral.** If you recall, a moral is a message of right and wrong that suggests how to behave.

There are themes in many kinds of texts. A **myth** may explain something about nature or a people. A **legend** is a tale from the past about people and events. It is usually connected to one time or place. A **folktale** is a story of regular people that contains a lesson about human behavior. A **fable** is a very short tale in which the characters may be animals with human traits. A **fairy tale** is a kind of story that involves magic or creatures, like fairies, interacting with humans.

Can you think of the themes in some stories you know? Have you seen the film *Pinocchio?* This is a fairy tale whose theme is "always tell the truth." In "The Tortoise and the Hare," you learn the lesson that "slow and steady wins the race."

Different kinds of stories will deal with many themes and topics. Each type of story can deal with a topic in a different way. There are many ways to tell similar types of stories.

Guided Practice

Read two passages. Then answer the questions.

immortal
to live forever

The Story of Hercules

In Roman myth, Hercules was the son of Jupiter. He was not a very smart man, but he was very, very brave. In fact, his bravery is what made him famous. He was also known for his sudden bursts of anger. Hercules had quite a temper! Yet, even though he was often mad, he always felt bad for his anger afterward. He accepted punishment for his actions.

Hercules was not born as a god. He started out as just a man. But, oh, what a strong man! In fact, when he was a baby, Hercules had two poisonous snakes in his crib with him. However, the snakes did not hurt him because he was able to defeat them before they bite him!

As a young man, Hercules still had trouble with his anger. One time, he just went too far in his anger. He was overcome by guilt afterwards, and did not know what to do. So, he talked to the king. The king told Hercules that if he completed 12 tasks, he would become immortal. The 12 tasks were difficult. Some people probably would have called them impossible. Yet, Hercules approached each task bravely, capturing monsters and overcoming great beasts. He finally completed the 12 tasks, and he became immortal. When Hercules's time on Earth was over, he became an immortal god—and he had become a hero.

Hercules's strength made him famous, but so did the lesson he had to learn. He had to learn the importance of using his great strength for good things. He also had to learn to control his temper! When he learned to do these things, he accomplished much.

The Story of Robin Hood

Have you heard of Robin Hood? His legend has been told and retold for centuries. Robin Hood was an outlaw. But many thought of him as a sort of hero. How could an outlaw be thought of as a hero? Well, that's an interesting story!

Deep in Sherwood Forest lived Robin Hood, dressed in green with a feather cap on his head. Robin Hood and his band of Merry Men would encounter people in the woods. They would then ask these people to join them for a meal. After a delicious meal, Robin Hood would ask these people how much money they had. If the people were truthful, there was no problem. As long as people were honest, they could keep everything they had. If people did not have enough money, Robin Hood would give them some. The only people that had to worry were those who lied. Robin Hood became angry with them because they were not truthful about how much money they had. When Robin Hood encountered these people, he would take their money and give it to people who did not have much.

Even though what Robin Hood did may be wrong, he was loved by many people. He lived by the rule of, "Rob from the rich and give to the poor." He was a friend to the poor and to those who were less fortunate.

How Robin Hood became an outlaw in the first place is a bit of a mystery. We do know that he was a master with a bow and arrow, and many legends claim that those abilities wound up getting him into trouble. He got into more than his fair share of fights! As the legend goes, Robin Hood did lose a couple fights. The people who beat him usually wound up joining his band of Merry Men. The band included Friar Tuck, Little John, and others. His group also included his true love, Maid Marian.

However Robin Hood became an outlaw, the story of this unusual hero lives on!

What type of character do *both* of these selections describe?

A a hero

B a monster

C a trickster

D a king

Hercules is described in the passage as doing things that are brave. He fought monsters and creatures. He was also very strong. Robin Hood gave to the poor. Otherwise, they would not have anything. These men were not monsters, tricksters, or kings. Both of these passages tell us that in some ways these men were heroes. Yet, they were not perfect. Choice A is the correct answer.

Compare the two passages. What three elements do they have in common?

_____

_____

_____

_____

These two passages share some common elements. Think about the main characters, their actions, and the type of story it is. Here is a sample answer:

Both passages are about men who did not always do everything right. However, they did things that were heroic. Both passages describe tales that have been around for a very long time. Finally, both men could be considered as not "good" because of some of their actions.

Contrast the two passages. What three elements are different?

_____

_____

_____

✔ The stories may both describe heroes, but they are not the same. Here is a sample answer:

Hercules is a myth, but Robin Hood is a legend. Hercules became a god. Robin Hood was an ordinary man. Robin Hood is not described as having the same physical strength that Hercules has.

Why might someone argue that Hercules and Robin Hood were *not* heroes?

_____

_____

_____

✔ It is hard to deny that both men did some good things. However, the passages also mention some things that aren't so admirable. Here is a sample answer:

Hercules has a bad temper. Robin Hood stole from people. Even though Hercules had guilt about his actions, he still did not always use his strength for good. Even though Robin Hood gave to the poor, he took things that did not belong to him.

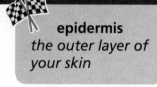

epidermis
*the outer layer of
your skin*

Fighting Germs

by Catherine Bevard

AH-CHOO! When you sneeze, many germs escape your body and spread through the air. In fact, there are many ways that germs can spread. How can we stop them from spreading?

The human body was designed to be a germ-fighter. For example, touch the skin on your arm. It probably feels warm and soft—but did you know that it is a germ-fighting layer? That skin is called your epidermis. It provides a barrier against germs. If you get hurt, make sure you wash your cut or scrape very well. It is important to keep those germs out of the wound, and your epidermis plays a large role in keeping you healthy!

There are things we can do to help our bodies trap germs. First, we should wash our hands! Do you notice that doctors always wash their hands and put on clean gloves before working with patients?

We should also be very careful with our food. When you have food left over after dinner, make sure it gets put away quickly. (You can offer to help your parents or guardians with this job!) The cold temperature in the refrigerator and the freezer slows down the growth of germs. Make sure that you wash surfaces that food has touched, whether that food has been cooked or not.

There are many types of germs, but the two most common are viruses and bacteria. Bacteria can multiply very quickly. The bacteria create waste, which is what makes you sick. Viruses are different. Viruses enter your body and create new viruses. Then they spread out, which makes you sick. That's when your body goes to work fighting those germs! Your body has special cells in its bloodstream that make up the immune system. These cells fight against the germs. Your body also produces special protein molecules in your blood called antibodies. Antibodies prepare your body to fight certain germs in the future.

However, you can do things to help fight germs before you ever get sick. Remember to stay away from people who are sick. Wash your hands. Eat healthy foods. Brush your teeth and get a lot of sleep! Make sure you go to the doctor and dentist regularly.

Germs will always be around, but the human body can fight them off—and you can help!

Jonas Salk

by Catherine Bevard

Over the years, many people have worked to prevent illnesses. Dr. Jonas Salk is one of these people. He helped to keep people from getting polio. Polio is an illness that can cause people to become paralyzed. Thanks to Dr. Jonas Salk, we do not really have to worry about getting this disease anymore.

Jonas Salk was born in New York. He studied medicine there, too. Salk did not treat people who were sick. Instead, he did research on how to prevent diseases. In fact, he discovered the first vaccine for polio.

Polio was a sickness that worried many people for a long time. Many children became ill from it. It infected thousands of people. Salk started working on the vaccine in 1947. It took him a long time to develop it. He tested it for many years. In 1955, the public started using the vaccine.

Once the public started using his vaccine, the number of children infected by polio in America went down by 90%. This man's work did not stop with this vaccine. He started the Salk Institute for Biological Studies. Today, this is still one of the leading places for disease and science research. Salk also wrote several books. He worked as a professor, too.

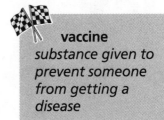

vaccine
substance given to prevent someone from getting a disease

Salk's parents did not work in medicine. However, his brothers did. One of his brothers was a veterinarian. The other, Lee, was a child psychologist. Lee did research on how a mother's heartbeat calms unborn children. Salk had three sons. His sons went into medicine and science, too.

Dr. Salk died in 1995. Yet, his work continues to make a difference in our lives today.

What subject do these two passages have in common?

A Both are about stopping illness.

B Both are about famous doctors.

C Both are about important scientists.

D Both are about keeping clean.

While both passages discuss health subjects, they do not both talk about doctors. They do not both talk about scientists. Only the first passage talks about keeping clean. However, both passages talk about preventing, or stopping, illness. The first passage discusses washing hands, for example. The second discusses vaccines. Both of these are ways to prevent illness. Choice A is the correct answer.

What is a *main* difference between these passages?

_____

_____

_____

_____

✓ **Both passages are about preventing illnesses. However, they discuss this topic in different ways. Here is a sample answer:**

> The first passage gives instructions. The author tells readers how to avoid germs. Also, the first passage explains how germs make us sick. The second text is a biography. It tells the reader about a person who worked in medicine to prevent illnesses. It does not discuss details about germs.

How do the two passages help you gain a better understanding of how to prevent sickness?

_____

_____

_____

_____

✓ **When you read more than one text, you learn more about a subject. Here is a sample answer:**

> If you just read one passage, you might say to wash your hands or get a shot to prevent sickness. Reading both shows the reader that there are many ways to stay healthy. Science gives us things like vaccines to keep us healthy. Our bodies have natural defenses built into them. We can do things like getting rest and washing hands to stay healthy, too. One would need to read both passages to get that information.

UNIT 4 ▨▨
Integration of Knowledge and Ideas

Test Yourself

Hofus the Stonecutter

a retelling of a Japanese folktale

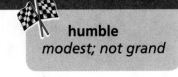

humble
modest; not grand

There once lived a poor stonecutter named Hofus. Every day, Hofus would go to work, and he would work very hard, from morning until night.

One day, though, Hofus delivered stones to a very rich man. When Hofus saw this man's home, he wished to himself, "Oh, I wish I could be as rich as this man!" Much to his surprise, a voice responded to his request. "Hofus," it said, "Be as wealthy as this man!" Suddenly, Hofus was very rich. When he returned to his home, where there once stood his small, humble hut, there now stood a large palace of gold.

Hofus decided he would not work anymore. He was happy, at first, but the days started to bore him. One day, when a golden carriage passed by his window, he thought, "How exciting it would be to be a prince, with an ornate carriage to ride in! Oh, I wish I could be a prince!" Again, the mysterious voice responded to Hofus. "Hofus," it said, "Be a prince!" And, so it was.

Hofus enjoyed being a prince, but that, too, began to grow old. So, he decided to make another transformation. When he looked out into the garden, he saw his flowers drooping, and he felt the sun burning him, in spite of his gorgeous, sheltering umbrellas. He realized the sun was very powerful. "Oh, I wish I could be the sun!" he said. That same, majestic voice replied. "Hofus," it said. "Be the sun!" And, so it was.

But soon, a cloud got in his way, and Hofus realized he was not completely powerful! "I wish," he said, "to be a cloud!" The voice responded, and Hofus was turned into a cloud. He poured rain down upon the land, but when he looked down upon his work, he realized that only the rocks stood unmoved by the flood he made. Hofus realized rocks were more powerful than he!

"I wish," Hofus yelled, "to be a rock!" He heard that voice again, and then was turned into a mighty, strong rock.

Hofus stayed content as a rock for awhile. One day, though, he felt a "tap! tap, tap!" at his feet. He looked down and saw a stonecutter. This stonecutter was slowly but surely breaking Hofus, the rock!

Something occurred to Hofus, then. He understood suddenly that there was something more powerful than a rock: a stonecutter.

And so, Hofus made his last wish. "I wish to be a stonecutter. I want to be myself again!" The voice responded, "Hofus, be yourself!" And, so it was. And Hofus never again wished to be anything but himself.

The Three Wishes

CHARACTERS:

Narrator

Husband

Mysterious Woman

Wife

ACT 1, Scene 1

NARRATOR: One gray, rainy day, a man was walking down the road toward his home when he came across a mysterious woman in a carriage. Her carriage was stuck in the mud, and it would not budge.

HUSBAND: Excuse me, may I assist you? Looks like you're pretty stuck!

MYSTERIOUS WOMAN: Yes, thank you!

HUSBAND: Let me give your carriage a bit of a push, and you'll soon be rolling along on your way.

MYSTERIOUS WOMAN: Thank you for your assistance, and now, I'd like to return the favor. What can I do to help you?

NARRATOR: The man immediately thought of his wife at home. They did not have much money, and he wanted to give his wife something to show his love for her.

HUSBAND: I have a wife at home. I would love it if you could do something to help her.

MYSTERIOUS WOMAN: Well, what if I told you I could grant her three wishes?

HUSBAND: That would be perfect!

NARRATOR: The man was overjoyed. He ran the rest of the way home, and he whistled as he walked through the door. His wife was in the kitchen, and he addressed her excitedly.

HUSBAND: You'll never guess what happened!

WIFE: What?

HUSBAND: I met the most mysterious woman on my way home. I helped her out, and she has graciously granted us three wishes. My dearest, I want to give those wishes to you!

WIFE: Oh, my goodness!

NARRATOR: The wife looked around their small, humble home and, then, she looked at the empty pan on their stove.

WIFE: There are many things I wish for, but right now, my wish is that we had some delicious sausage for dinner!

NARRATOR: Like magic, a sausage appeared in the pan, and they prepared to feast on it. The wife put the sausage on the plates but, then, the husband clumsily knocked the plates over.

WIFE: Oh, no! Look what you've done, you! I wish that sausage were on your nose, you silly man!

NARRATOR: The woman clapped her hand over her mouth to silence herself, but it was too late. The man now had a sausage instead of a nose!

HUSBAND: Look what you did! What in the world are we going to do now? We have wasted two wishes—and do I even need to mention my ridiculous new nose?

WIFE: Why don't you just remove it from your face?

HUSBAND: I can't! It seems to be stuck!

WIFE: Well, we don't have any other choice, do we?

HUSBAND: No, we don't… I don't see any way to remove this sausage from my face except to wish it away.

WIFE: Well, then, here goes. I wish for the sausage to once again be back on our plates for supper!

NARRATOR: Well, she got her final wish, and the two had a wonderful meal…but nothing more. They had already exhausted their wishes. And, they learned a valuable lesson. They never fought again, and they were forever careful about what they wished for!

1 Which of the following describe *both* "Hofus the Stonecutter" and "The Three Wishes"?

   A They are true stories.

   B They teach lessons.

   C They are by the same author.

   D They both include husbands.

2 Explain your answer to question 1.

_____

_____

_____

_____

3 Which of these *best* describes the lesson in both "Hofus the Stonecutter" and "The Three Wishes"?

A Be kind to others.

B Always be prepared.

C Be careful what you wish for.

D Pay attention to mystery forces.

4 Explain your answer to question 3.

_____

_____

_____

_____

_____

UNIT 4 ▨▨▨▨▨▨▨▨▨▨▨▨▨▨▨▨▨▨▨▨▨▨▨▨▨
Integration of Knowledge and Ideas

5 What is similar and what is different about how the authors present their stories?

_____

_____

_____

_____

6 Compare how Hofus in "Hofus the Stonecutter" and the husband and wife in "The Three Wishes" waste their wishes.

_____

_____

_____

_____

REVIEW

Integration of Knowledge and Ideas

Vocabulary
famine
gourd
iceberg
Orient

Read two passages. Then answer the questions.

The Endless Tale

There once lived an extraordinarily rich man who had a daughter who was an incredible storyteller. The daughter's father enjoyed her stories so much that he wished for her to never marry. He wanted to keep her around to tell him these fantastic stories. He wanted to listen to her tales forever.

"I wish your stories would go on forever," he said. "Or, at least, I wish they could each go on for a month!"

"Don't be silly, father!" the daughter exclaimed. "Stories that go on for a month would be very boring."

"Surely, they would not!" said the father. "In fact, I believe that is so impossible, that if anyone could ever tell me a month-long story that bored me, I would let him marry you!"

This news quickly traveled throughout the daughter's small village. The young men in the village all worked tirelessly to invent fantastic, long stories to tell the rich man. The rich man's daughter, though, had fallen in love with one man. However, this man was poor. The daughter knew her father would not let her marry him. Therefore, she told him what to say when he told his story.

The man came to see the father to tell him the month-long story. The story was about a rich, wise man who harvested all his corn and hid it in a cave because he thought a famine might come. The man in the story did not see a tiny crack in the cave's wall, so he did not notice an ant that came in and began to steal the corn. "And then the ant came back and stole another grain of corn," the boy said. "And then, he stole another grain. And then, he stole another grain. And then he stole another grain…" the boy continued to say this, over and over. Well, the man in the story had thousands upon thousands of grains of corn, so this story could go on forever!

After three days of telling this story, the rich man spoke up. "You win!" he said. "This story is boring me to tears!"

The poor boy smiled. "But, sir, the story is not nearly over."

The rich man laughed, in spite of the situation, and said, "I know when I am beat! You may have my daughter's hand in marriage. That is the most boring tale I have ever heard!"

Water, Water Will Be Mine

Long, long ago, there was a stretch of time in which there was no rain. The rivers, oceans, and creeks dried up. The world's animals had nothing to drink. They all had to band together and ask each other, "What will we do? We have no water to drink!" The crocodiles no longer swam in the water, and the leopard ate dust instead of drinking water. The waterbuck and the warthog longed for liquid; they were truly parched. The animals had a meeting at which they decided they must dig deep into the earth, because that was where they would find water. They all decided to work together, whether they usually got along or not.

Well… they all decided to work together, except for one animal. The rabbit decided that he did not want to dig. He wanted to watch instead. The animals told him, "Rabbit, if you do not dig, you cannot have water!" However, the rabbit laughed and told them that he would have water whether he dug or not.

Finally, the animals dug deep enough to find water. "Water, water will be mine!" they chanted. The animals drank until they were satisfied, then they all went to bed.

When they awoke the next day, there were fresh footprints in the dirt around the water. They knew whose footprints they were. "Rabbit!" they cried. "We told you that if you did not dig, you do not drink!" The angry animals decided that they must have someone guard the water hole. They chose the monkey for this task. The monkey guarded the water hole and, sure enough, along came that rabbit!

"Get away, rabbit!" cried the monkey. "You did not dig; you cannot drink!"

"Why would I want to drink that dirty water?" said the rabbit. "I have this water here, which is as sweet as honey!" The rabbit held up a gourd.

"Sweet as honey?" the curious monkey replied. "Where did you get that water?"

"Don't you worry about that," said the rabbit. "Would you like to try?" The monkey gave into temptation. He drank and drank—and as he drank from the rabbit's gourd, the rabbit snuck over to the water hole and drank again. And, no matter who guarded the water hole, the rabbit outsmarted him with his gourd. That clever rabbit won every time!

gourd
a plant with a hard shell that is used to drink water from

1 "The Endless Tale" and "Water, Water Will Be Mine" both feature main characters who _____.

A trick someone

B find true love

C win a race

D teach a lesson

2 "The Endless Tale" and "Water, Water Will Be Mine" both are _____.

A fables

B myths

C legends

D folktales

UNIT 4 ▚▚▚▚▚▚▚▚▚▚▚▚▚▚▚▚▚▚▚▚▚▚▚▚▚▚▚▚▚▚▚▚▚▚
Integration of Knowledge and Ideas

3 Explain your answers to questions 1 and 2.

_____

_____

_____

_____

_____

4 How does the daughter in "The Endless Tale" differ from the rabbit in "Water, Water Will Be Mine"?

_____

_____

_____

_____

_____

5 What are two things that are similar between these two passages?

_____

_____

_____

_____

_____

6 What is different between the two passages?

_____

_____

_____

_____

_____

Passage 1

Titanic

On April 12, 1912, the largest ship ever built set sail. This ship was named the *Titanic*. It was built in Ireland. It left Southampton, England, with more than 2,000 people on board. This was one of the most important events in history. The ship was almost 900 feet long. Four days after the *Titanic* left the harbor, it struck an iceberg and sank. Only 700 people survived. How could this happen? How did the ship sink?

We now know that several warnings came in to the ship about the iceberg. The ship tried to avoid the dangers of ice, but it could not.

Because of its size, the *Titanic* could not easily move around the ice. Icebergs are not just small pieces of ice. They are often pieces of glaciers floating in the ocean. Only about $\frac{1}{9}$ of the ice shows above water. The rest is a large mass of ice below the surface. Thus, it was almost impossible for the *Titanic's* captain to know how much ice was below the water's surface.

Another problem was that the *Titanic* did not carry enough lifeboats. Everyone believed the *Titanic* was unsinkable, so the ship's builders did not think they needed to have enough lifeboats for everyone on board. When the *Titanic* sank, the lifeboats could not hold all the people on board the *Titanic*.

iceberg
a large mass of ice that has separated from a glacier

Passage 2

Nuestra Señora de la Concepción

In 1638, there was a famous shipwreck. The ship that sank was called the *Nuestra Señora de la Concepción*. At that time, the *Concepción* was the largest ship that had been built. It was somewhere between 140 and 160 feet long. Bad weather is believed to have caused the shipwreck.

This ship was carrying about 400 people, and many of them perished in this wreck. The ship was also carrying a large shipment of cargo. This included fine silks and rugs from the Orient and gold and silver. The cargo was worth a great deal of money. The loss of this ship was expensive to Spain. Jewels and other treasures were lost when the jars holding them were lost in the deep sea. In fact, over a thousand pieces of jewelry were lost.

Orient
countries in the Far East

186 UNIT 4 ▨▨▨▨▨▨▨▨▨▨▨▨▨▨▨▨▨▨▨▨▨▨▨▨▨▨▨▨
Integration of Knowledge and Ideas

There is still disagreement over the loss of the ship and its treasure. Some people say the ship's captain was too young and inexperienced. Others just blame the weather. The ship was tossed against rock, and it was thrown against coral. It did not stand a chance. The wreck made large holes in the ship. The ship's contents spilled from these holes and were lost at sea. There was also no record of what was lost because the ship sailed without reporting its inventory.

7 Determine which of these statements from passage 1 is an opinion.

   A The ship was almost 900 feet long.

   B Four days after the *Titanic* left the harbor, it struck an iceberg and sank.

   C This was one of the most important events in history.

   D The lifeboats could not hold all the people on board the *Titanic*.

8 Examine the illustration with passage 1. What does it help you understand about the passage?

   A Icebergs are very small.

   B Icebergs are easy to see.

   C It is hard to tell how large an iceberg is.

   D The *Titanic* should have been able to avoid the iceberg.

9 Provide an example of an opinion from passage 2.

_____

_____

_____

_____

10 Analyze the two passages. How are they similar?

_____

_____

_____

_____

_____

11 Identify three facts from passage 1.

_____

_____

_____

_____

_____

12 Identify three facts from passage 2.

_____

_____

_____

_____

_____

PRACTICE TEST

Vocabulary

Civil War
Confederate
lieutenant
mortar
musket
pestle

The Red Badge of Courage

by Stephen Crane

an adaptation

When he woke from dozing, the young soldier struggled to see. He rubbed his eyes and squinted, trying to make out the shapes in the dark. The dying fire silhouetted the tall trees above them, and muddy grass carpeted the ground beneath. He could see small groups of men spread out, sleeping in the shadows. Their faces glowed in the low firelight, looking ghostlike. But the young soldier had no fear. After the long day's battle, the men slept hard. Arms and legs sprawled in every direction, but a few pairs of legs stuck out stiff and straight. Shoes were caked with mud and weeds and trousers were torn from running through fields.

On the other side of the fire, the boy could see an exhausted officer knocked out. The man was sitting up straight, eyes closed, his back leaning against a tree, his body swaying back and forth like a doddering old man. His face was covered with dirt, and his jaw hung open. His uniform was frayed and stained. His once-gleaming sword lay on the ground beside him.

Once in a while, a soldier would stir. He might turn his body to find a new position on the ground or suddenly sit up and look at the fire in confusion. He would glance over to his buddy and grunt. Then he would lie down to sleep again.

The young soldier's eyes grew heavy, and he began to nod. The place where the bullet had grazed his head still throbbed in pain. He picked up his blankets, spread one out on the ground and wrapped the other around his shoulders. Then, at last, he stretched out on the ground. It felt as soft as a thick feather bed. The warmth and softness made him sigh as his head fell to his elbow. As his eyelids covered his eyes, with a sigh, he snuggled into his blankets. In seconds, he was sound asleep.

1 The word <u>silhouetted</u> means _____.

   A blew onto

   B cast a shadow

   C hugged tightly

   D moved quickly

2 Read this sentence from the passage.

     It felt as soft as a thick feather bed.

  This is an example of _____.

   A a metaphor

   B a simile

   C alliteration

   D onomatopoeia

3 In paragraph 2, the idiom <u>knocked out</u> means _____.

   A hit

   B tired

   C awake

   D asleep

4 Read this sentence from the passage.

     He might turn his body to find a new position on the ground or suddenly sit up and look at the fire in confusion.

  Which of these is the *best* meaning of the word <u>position</u> as it is used in the sentence?

   A location

   B posture

   C rank

   D opinion

Practice Test

5 The officer is described as <u>exhausted</u>. What is the officer *most likely* feeling?

   A   like he is full of energy

   B   like his body has not rested for weeks

   C   like his body has no feeling

   D   like the weight of the world on his shoulders

Read the poem. Then answer the questions.

Tenting Tonight

by Walter Kittredge, 1864

We're tenting tonight on the old camp-ground
Give us a song to cheer
Our weary hearts, a song of home
And friends we love so dear.

Repeat chorus

5   We've been tenting tonight on the old camp-ground,
Thinking of days gone by
Of the loved ones at home that gave us the hand,
And the tear that said, "Good-by!"

Repeat chorus

We are tired of war on the old camp-ground;
10 Many are the dead and gone
Of the brave and true who've left their homes;
Others been wounded long.

Repeat chorus

We've been fighting today on the old camp-ground,
Many are lying near;
15 Some are dead, and some are dying,
Many are in tears.

Chorus

Many are the hearts that are weary tonight,
Wishing for the war to cease;
Many are the hearts looking for the light,
20 To see the dawn of peace.
Dying tonight, dying tonight,
Dying on the old camp-ground.

6 Determine the structure of "Tenting Tonight."

    A acts and scenes

    B sentences and paragraphs

    C chorus and verses

    D chapters

7 Who is the speaker in "Tenting Tonight"?

    A Walter Kittredge

    B the soldiers' wives

    C the soldiers' sons

    D the soldiers

8 Interpret what the author means by "many are the hearts."

    A weary, homesick soldiers

    B rows of military tents

    C long days of war

    D tears and sadness

9 Analyze "The Red Badge of Courage" and "Tenting Tonight."
How are they similar? How are they different?

_____

_____

_____

_____

_____

Practice Test

Johnny Clem

Did you know that boys under the age of 18 fought in war? During the Civil War, more than 10,000 boys served in the Union army. The youngest was John Lincoln "Johnny" Clem. Johnny was born in Newark, Ohio, in 1851. His parents named him John Joseph Klem. When Johnny was 9 years old, he ran away from home to join the army.

First, Johnny tried to join the Ohio unit as the soldiers went through his hometown. They laughed at him because he was only 9 years old. He was turned down again when he tried to join the Michigan unit. Johnny would not give up. He followed them as their drummer boy. Finally, Johnny was allowed to work around the army's camp. The officers paid him $13 a month. They gave him a small uniform and a shortened musket. Newspaper reporters named him the "smallest drummer." During one battle in Tennessee, Johnny's drum was smashed by enemy fire. Finally, in 1863, Johnny was allowed to join the army. He was 12 years old.

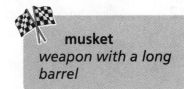

musket
weapon with a long barrel

Johnny entered the Battle of Chickamauga. He carried only his musket. A Confederate officer tried to capture him. Johnny got away. He was named the "Drummer Boy of Chickamauga." The newspapers loved to tell stories about him. Johnny soon became commander. Then he changed his name to John Lincoln Clem.

In October 1863, Johnny was captured. The enemy made an example of him. The Confederates said the Union army was poor. They said that they were sending "babies" out to fight. By late 1864, Johnny left the army.

Johnny tried to attend West Point. However, he had little education and was not accepted. In 1871, President Grant made him a lieutenant. Later, Johnny became a high-ranking officer. Johnny Clem lived to be 85 years old. He died in 1937 and was buried at Arlington National Cemetery. He is a true American hero.

lieutenant
military office below captain

10 Analyze the structure of this passage. How is the information in this passage organized?

    A cause and effect

    B problem and solution

    C compare and contrast

    D events in time order

11 What is the main idea of "Johnny Clem"?

    A Children should serve in the military.

    B Johnny Clem was one of the youngest Civil War soldiers.

    C The Union army should have sent Johnny home.

    D Johnny did not have good parents.

12 Which of the following is true about the events in Johnny Clem's life?

    A Johnny joined the Union army, tried to attend West Point, was captured by the enemy, then ran away.

    B Johnny tried to attend West Point, ran away, was captured by the enemy, then joined the Union army.

    C Johnny ran away, joined the Union army, was captured by the enemy, then tried to attend West Point.

    D Johnny was captured by the enemy, joined the Union army, tried to attend West Point, then ran away.

13 Analyze the passage. What can you infer about Johnny Clem's character?

_____

_____

_____

_____

_____

14 Identify an example of an opinion used in "Johnny Clem."

_____

_____

_____

_____

_____

Read the two folktales. Then answer the questions.

The Flea

a traditional Mexican folktale

There once lived a brilliant magician. He had a daughter, whom he loved very much. Now, this daughter fell in love with a boy and asked her father if the two could be married. Her father, always protective of his daughter, said, "If he can outsmart me, you can marry him." Turning to the boy, the magician said, "If you can sleep for three nights where my spells cannot find you, then you can marry her." The magician was smug. This was not the first time that someone had tried to outsmart him!

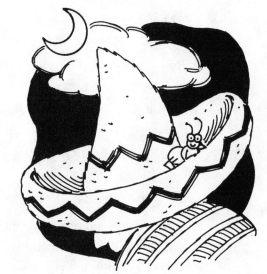

What the father did not know was that this boy was also a magician! The first night, the boy tried to sleep cradled on the moon. But the next day, the older magician said, "It cannot be comfortable to sleep on the moon."

The boy was, perplexed. He had always thought himself a mighty smart fellow! How had the older magician known where he was? The next night, the boy tried to sleep inside a shell, hidden deep in the dark blue sea. But the magician found him yet again! It seemed like the boy might not win this contest.

The boy thought hard. What could he do? Then he had a fantastic idea! He snuck outside and turned himself into a tiny flea. Then he waited… and waited… and waited. Finally, just when he was about to give up on his plan, the magician came outside, and he jumped onto the rim of the magician's sombrero. Surely, he would not find the boy now!

The magician looked high and low for the boy. He looked absolutely everywhere! He couldn't understand how he could be tricked. (He certainly didn't realize that the boy was sitting on top of his hat!) Finally, he gave up looking, and decided to find the boy the next day. When the magician went inside, the flea hopped down from the hat onto the door jam and settled down for a good night of much-needed rest. He repeated this for the next three nights and, each night, the magician wandered around, inside and out, searching for this very clever boy.

On the third day, the flea turned back into the boy. He walked through the door of the house and addressed the magician. The magician simply shook his head in wonder. "You have outsmarted me," he said.

The Clever Daughter
a traditional folktale

There once lived a peasant and his daughter. They lived a simple life, in a small house, and they wanted desperately to improve their lives. One day, the daughter had an idea. "Father," she said, "why don't we ask the king for some land? We could really improve our lives and make some money if we started farming!"

The father thought that this was a great idea. "Yes," he responded, "I think you have quite a fantastic idea, there!" So, the two went to the king, who graciously granted their request.

The two farmed their land, day in and day out. One sweltering day, while working, they came across a mortar made of gold. The father excitedly exclaimed, "The king has been kind to us. We should present this mortar to him as a sign of our gratitude."

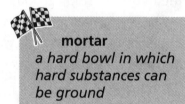

mortar
a hard bowl in which hard substances can be ground

"But, Father," the daughter responded, "if we do not give him a golden pestle, he will think we stole it! One never sees a mortar without its pestle!" The daughter was very worried, but the father disagreed with her. Disregarding his daughter's concern, he took the golden mortar to the king.

When the king saw it, he asked, "But where is the pestle? Why do you bring me only part of what you found? You are being extremely dishonest, even after I have been so generous to you!" Too late, the father realized his daughter had been right, and he was sentenced to spend a long time in prison.

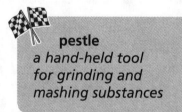

pestle
a hand-held tool for grinding and mashing substances

The father begged and pleaded with the king. "My daughter warned me that this would happen," he said. "She told me not to bring you this, because she knew that I would be accused of theft and sentenced to time in jail." The saddened father buried his head in his hands and wept.

"Your daughter sounds so very clever. Tell her to come see me," came the king's response. The next time the daughter visited her father, he pleaded with her to go and visit the king.

Practice Test

When she saw the king, he said to her, "I hear you are quite clever. I will give you a riddle, and if you can solve it, your father will be free."

"That is fair," said the daughter. "What is the riddle?"

"Tomorrow," said the king, "Come to the palace. Be clothed, but unclothed. Do not be riding, and do not be walking. You must come partially on the road, but partially off it."

So, the next day, the daughter came to the palace wrapped in a fishnet. She tied the fishnet to a donkey, so that she was pulled to the castle—not walking or riding. She touched her toes to the ground as she was pulled, so that she was partially on the road and partially off.

The king was impressed. "I am a man who stays true to his promises, and what's fair is fair," he said. "Your father is free."

15 What do the boy in "The Flea" and the daughter in "The Clever Daughter" have in common?

A good looks

B jealousy

C cleverness

D hard workers

16 What theme do these two stories have in common?

A Cleverness wins out in the end.

B Honesty is the best policy.

C Slow and steady wins the race.

D Be careful what you wish for.

17 Give evidence from the two passages to support your answer to question 16.

_____

_____

_____

_____

_____

18 Predict what will _most likely_ happen next in "The Flea."

_____

_____

_____

_____

_____

Read two passages. Then answer the questions.

Passage 1

Letter to the Principal: Healthy Lunches

Dear Mrs. Valdez,

My name is Julie, and I am in fourth grade here at Jefferson Elementary School. I am very worried about the lunches I see my classmates eating, and I think some things need to change. We need to have new rules about healthy lunches.

Candy. Potato chips. Soda. French fries. It seems like every school lunch I see is full of unhealthy food! My friends always have so much junk food in their lunches! Eating an unhealthy lunch is not good for you. It will make you lose energy, and it will not help you focus on your work. Students should only have healthy food in their lunches.

Have you ever noticed that many students drink soda pop instead of water or juice? This is bad for our teeth, and the sugar does not do anything good for us! Instead of soda, students should drink juice or other nutritious drinks. Or, they should drink water. Water is very good for us!

Practice Test

Mrs. Valdez, I know that many students buy their lunches here at school. For those students, there should only be healthy options. I do not think we should have hot dogs, hamburgers, or pizza available. Or, if we do, we should also have salads and vegetables with them. I know that everyone's favorite part of lunch is the unhealthy stuff. But, as our parents tell us, we have to eat the healthy foods, too!

I know that you care about the students here at Jefferson. You always say "hello!" to us with a smile, and you are always interested in what we are up to. So, I knew that I could bring this concern to you. I know that you want students to be healthy. Will you please make new rules about student lunches so that we can all be healthier? Thank you!

Sincerely,

Julie Brown

Passage 2

School Uniforms: An Editorial

There is much talk about school uniforms. Some students argue that it is not fair to make them wear uniforms, but many people see school uniforms as a good thing.

Why do people see them as a good thing? First, they can create a feeling of school spirit. Uniforms can provide a sense of unity in students. Also, there is less risk of students feeling left out because they are not wearing something cool. Instead of looking at what is on the outside, students can really get to know each other. They will not judge each other based on clothes.

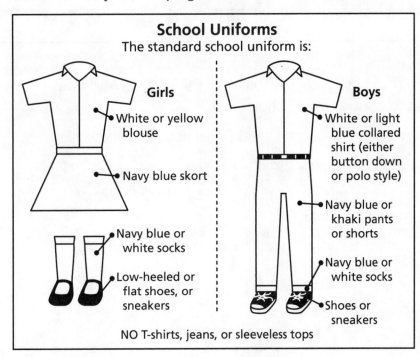

School Uniforms
The standard school uniform is:

Girls
- White or yellow blouse
- Navy blue skort
- Navy blue or white socks
- Low-heeled or flat shoes, or sneakers

Boys
- White or light blue collared shirt (either button down or polo style)
- Navy blue or khaki pants or shorts
- Navy blue or white socks
- Shoes or sneakers

NO T-shirts, jeans, or sleeveless tops

In 2000, a poll of public school principals showed that 12% of public schools require students to wear uniforms. About 55% of public school principals said that their schools have a "very strict" dress code.

School uniforms make it easier for teachers to focus on teaching. If students wear the same clothing, then teachers do not have to make sure students are dressed appropriately. They can spend class time teaching.

Uniforms help students learn important things. Students will see that it does not matter how much money people have or what kind of clothes they wear. Uniforms help students see each other for who they are. They help students to not judge each other based on how much their clothes cost. Students will not form little groups based on clothing style. Instead, they will focus on their shared interests.

All students should wear uniforms. This is the best way to make sure that students get along well. It is also the best way to make sure that they focus on what really matters and not on clothing. Students can wear the clothes they want to wear on the weekends. When they are in school, they should all wear the same thing.

19 What does the diagram used to illustrate passage 2 help you understand about the passage?

_____

_____

_____

_____

_____

20 Analyze passage 1 and its photograph. Which of these sentences from passage 1 is *best* supported by the photograph?

A It seems like every school lunch I see is full of unhealthy food!

B I know that you want students to be healthy.

C Instead of soda, students should drink juice or other nutritious drinks.

D But, as our parents tell us, we have to eat the healthy foods, too!

21 In passage 1, do you think Julie Brown supports her argument with enough facts? Why or why not?

_____

_____

_____

_____

_____

22 How does the author of passage 2 use evidence to support her argument?

_____

_____

_____

_____

_____

Read the passage. Then answer the questions.

Pet Dinosaur

It has always been my dream to have a dinosaur for a pet. I asked and asked, but it never failed, my mom and dad always said, "No." I didn't know why they couldn't understand how amazing it would be! Didn't they realize they would benefit, too, if we had a dinosaur as a pet? Sure, our family dog, Mazey, was part of our family, but she wasn't really capable of doing many of the things a pet dinosaur could do.

I first had this brilliant idea for a pet dinosaur when we studied them in science class. They were so interesting! I rushed home from school to tell my parents all I had learned. That's when I first asked them if I could have a pet dinosaur?

"A dinosaur?" my mom shrieked. "For a pet?"

"Yeah, it would make the perfect pet and companion," I explained. "I even named my pet dinosaur. It would be named Chonos. In Greek mythology, he is the old and wise god of time."

I had already decided that if I asked for a pet dinosaur, it would have to be an herbivore. Herbivores eat plants. I knew we would be safe with a plant-eating dinosaur. I knew my mom would have said "no" right way if I asked for a carnivore like *T. rex*. Even I knew we might get hurt with a meat-eating dinosaur in our house. Who's to say we wouldn't become dinner some day?

Then I told them all the tasks a dinosaur would be able to help us with. It would help Dad by cutting, or eating, the lawn. I mean, it is a plant-eater! Dad wouldn't have to mow the lawn. It could take my sister and me to school. My mom would save time and gas. Who wouldn't like to make a positive impact on the environment? When my mom and dad wanted to go out to dinner with their friends, we'd have a babysitter. They would no longer have to try to find one that was available, and then pay him. They'd save money, and we'd have a fantastic time! Plus, if we saw our dinosaur eating vegetables all the time, I'm sure my sister and I would eat more of ours and stop complaining when Mom asked us to eat more. Our dinosaur would set a good example for us. A dinosaur would make the perfect pet for many reasons!

After relaying all these wonderful ideas, Mom and Dad still weren't convinced.

"Did you hear anything I just said?" I asked. "A pet dinosaur would be the best thing ever!"

"A dinosaur would be a lot of work, and you don't always feed Mazey without being reminded—constantly," Mom said.

"You have made a great case for having a dinosaur for a pet," Dad said. "It's very convincing. But…"

"I know, I know," I answered sullenly. "How could I have a pet dinosaur when they have been extinct for millions of years?"

23 Which of these *best* describes what this story is about?

    A Convincing your parents to get a new pet takes hard work.

    B Learning about dinosaurs is important.

    C You should always do your best.

    D Don't ask anyone else to solve your problems for you.

24 Why did the main character think a dinosaur would make a better pet than Mazey?

    A Mazey was old.

    B Mazey couldn't run.

    C Mazey didn't like to go out for walks.

    D Mazey couldn't do many of the things a dinosaur could do.

25 Which of the following words is *most likely* related to Chronos, the Greek god of time?

    A chronological

    B herculean

    C narcissistic

    D July

A New Dream

Madison couldn't believe it—she didn't make the cast of the community center play. She had been acting for as long as she could remember. She was never the star, but she had always been cast in some role, however small. This year she wasn't even picked for a small role. What was she going to do now? It was time to find a new hobby, but she couldn't decide what.

As she sulked into the kitchen, Madison's mom looked up from the newspaper. Seeing her youngest daughter upset was not easy for her mom. Madison knew this.

"What's wrong?" Mom asked. "I know you are still upset about the play, but moping around the house the entire summer is not going to help."

"I know, Mom," Madison said. "I just don't know what to do. I'm not really good at anything else."

"That's not true," Mom reminded her. "You are an excellent student, you care about your family and friends, and you are very responsible."

"Thanks, but you are only saying those things because you are my mom. You have to," Madison let out a little smile.

"Look here," Mom said pointing to an ad in the newspaper. "There is an art show featuring local artists tomorrow afternoon. Why don't we check it out? It will be fun!"

"Alright," Madison sighed. "It's not like I have anything else to do."

The next day, as they walked into the old building, they were surrounded by art of all kinds. Photographs, paintings, abstract art, pottery, and jewelry were all around them. Madison hardly knew where to start.

They approached a booth that held beautiful photographs of wildlife and people. Madison couldn't take her eyes off them.

"Well, hello!" a young woman said. "I'm Betsy. Thanks for coming to see my work," she smiled and held out her hand to introduce herself.

"Your work is stunning," Mom said. "How did you get started in photography?"

Betsy explained that as a young girl, her grandfather had given her one of his old cameras for her birthday. He taught her how to use it, and she began taking pictures of everything that was around her—trees, flowers, birds, squirrels, her dog, and her family.

Madison held Mom's hand as she left the art exhibit. She thought to herself, "I feel a new dream growing in my heart."

26 What will be Madison's new dream? Explain how you know.

_____

_____

_____

_____

_____

27 What specific event caused Madison to go to the art show?

A She didn't get a part in the play.

B She couldn't go to the play.

C She loved photography.

D She wanted to meet Betsy.

28 Which of these would *not* be included in a summary of the story?

A Madison needed to find a new hobby.

B Madison wore a dress to the art show.

C Madison and her mom went to an art show.

D An artist told Madison how she began taking pictures.

29 Madison didn't know what kind of a hobby she should try because ____.

    A they didn't have money for her to take any classes

    B she didn't think she was good at anything other than acting

    C she only liked acting

    D she had tried so many things already

30 Analyze the point of views used in "Pet Dinosaur" and in "A New Dream." How are they same or different?

_____

_____

_____

_____

_____

GLOSSARY

A

Alliteration	repeating the same consonant sounds
Antonyms	words with an opposite meaning
Aroma	the smell of food being cooked
Asthma	an illness that makes it difficult to breathe

B

Ballad	narrative poem originally written to be sung
Battery	container in which chemical energy is made into electricity and used as a power source

C

Chrysalis	cocoon of an insect
Civil War	war between the northern and southern states of the U.S.
Climax	the high point of the story
Confederate	the southern forces that fought to break away from the U.S.
Consistent	reliable; steady
Couplet	two lines that rhyme in a poem
Creatures	living things
Crystalline Rock	rock made of crystallized matter
Cuisine	style of cooking and preparing food
Culture	ways of people in our family, community, and country

D

Dawning	beginning to appear
Definitions	words that tell what another word means
Descriptions	words that tell you more about another word
Detour	a forced change in direction

Docked		money taken from pay for being late or for bad behavior
Dumb		someone or something that cannot talk

E

Edible	fit to be eaten
Editor	person who is in charge and decides the final content of a text
Embarrassing	causing someone to feel self-conscious
Epidermis	outer layer of your skin
Exhilaration	act of being excited or thrilled
Exploration	act of traveling to discover more about a new place

F

Famine	lack of food
Flashback	events that happened at an earlier time
Foreman	boss
Foreshadowing	suggestion that some event is to occur in the future
Free verse	poem that does not rhyme or have a rhythm

G

Genre	type of literature
Gourd	a plant with a hard shell that is used to drink from
Grenadier	a soldier

H

Haiku	Japanese 17-syllable poem usually written in three lines
Harvested	brought in or gathered crops
Haunting	repeating
Homographs	words that are spelled the same but that have different meanings
Humble	modest; not grand
Hyperbole	exaggerated statement for effect

I

Iceberg	a large mass of ice that has separated from a glacier
Idioms	phrase that means something other than the literal meaning

Immigrant	person who leaves his own country to live in another country
Immortal	to live forever
Inca	South American Indian people living in the Central Andes before the Spanish conquest
Intensity	degree of strength or power
Intersections	places where two roads come together and cross
Invading	entering another country with the purpose of taking it over

L

Ladybird	a type of red and black spotted beetle, also known as a ladybug
Landfills	areas where trash and garbage are buried to build up low-lying land
Laser	device that creates a powerful beam of light
Lieutenant	military office below rank of captain
Limerick	humorous rhyming five-line poem
Lyric Poem	a poem that expresses the poet's feelings

M

Metaphor	type of figurative language that compares two unlike things but does not use *like* or *as*
Molt	shed outer covering
Mortar	hard bowl in which hard substances can be ground
Musket	weapon with a long barrel

N

Narrative Poem	a poem that tells a story
Nonrenewable	something that cannot be used again because there is only so much of it available

O

Onomatopoeia	words that sound like what they are describing
Orient	countries in the Far East
Overland	by, on, or across land

P

Panic	sudden fear for no reason
Parched	dry, or thirsty
Personification	giving human characteristics to a concept or inanimate object
Pesticides	chemicals sprayed on crops to keep bugs away
Pestle	hand-held tool for grinding and mashing substances
Plateau	land area raised above the earth, with a flat top
Point of View	who is telling the story
first-person	the main character is telling the story; uses first person pronouns *I* and *we*
third-person limited omniscient	narrator is limited to knowledge of the thoughts and feelings of only one of the characters; uses third-person pronouns *he, she,* and *they*
third-person omniscient	outside narrator is all-knowing and can reveal the thoughts and feelings of more than one of the characters; uses third-person pronouns *he, she,* and *they*
Prefix	part of a word added to beginning of another word that changes the meaning of the word
Premature	too early

Q

Quill	hollow shaft of a feather used to write with when dipped in ink

R

Renewable	something that can be used or renewed again because there is plenty of it
Rhyme	repeated sounds at the ends of words
Rhythm	pattern of stressed and unstressed beat in a line of poetry
Rival	someone competing to be the best at something, such as winning a sports game
Routine	follow the same steps over and over

S

Scythe	a tool used to cut grass or crops, such as wheat
Sedimentary Rock	rock formed by mineral and organic matter

Simile	type of figurative language that compares two unlike things using *as* or *like*
Snatched	reached or grabbed
Stanza	a group of lines within a poem, similar to a chapter within a book
Suffix	part of a word added to the end of another word that changes the meaning of the word
Summit	highest point
Synonyms	words that have a similar meaning

T

Tarriers	Irish workers whose job was to drill holes in rock to blast out railroad tunnels
Tay	tea
Tenement	building in the poorer part of a city that has apartments or rooms for rent
Toll	a charge or fee for use
Tsunami	many waves that come after an earthquake or other disturbance under the sea
Tunic	long, tight-fitting jacket with a collar
Turnstile	a post with revolving horizontal bars placed at an entrance to allow one person to pass through at a time
Twilight	faint light in the sky between sunset and darkness

V

Vaccine	substance given to prevent someone from getting a disease
Volcano	mountain or hill with a crater or vent through which lava, rock, and gas may erupt from Earth's crust

W

Wayfarers	people who travel on foot
Work Camp	a prison camp of workers

NOTES

NOTES